Doctor Who: Volume 3

CHAPTER 1: SPACE SQUID

WRITTEN BY TONY LEE
ART BY JOSH ADAMS
COLORS BY RACHELLE ROSENBERG

CHAPTER 2: BODY SNATCHED

WRITTEN BY TONY LEE
ART BY MATTHEW DOW SMITH
COLORS BY CHARLIE KIRCHOFF

CHAPTER 3: SILENT KNIGHT

WRITTEN BY TONY LEE
ART BY PAUL GRIST
COLORS BY PHIL ELLIOTT

CHAPTER 4: RUN, DOCTOR, RUN

WRITTEN BY JOSHUA HALE FIALKOV
ART BY BLAIR SHEDD

CHAPTER 5: DOWN TO EARTH

WRITTEN BY MATTHEW DOW SMITH
ART BY MITCH GERADS
COLORS BY MITCH GERADS AND KYLE LATINO

CHAPTER 6: TUESDAY

STORY, ART, AND COLORS BY DAN MCDAID
COLORS ASSIST BY DEBORAH MCCUMISKEY

LETTERING BY SHAWN LEE AND NEIL UYETAKE

ORIGINAL SERIES EDITS BY DENTON J. TIPTON

COLLECTION COVER BY BLAIR SHEDD WITH MITCH GERADS, DAN MCDAID, JOSH ADAMS, AND RACHELLE ROSENBERG

COLLECTION EDITS BY JUSTIN EISINGER AND ALONZO SIMON

COLLECTION DESIGN BY CHRIS MOWRY

Special thanks to Kate Bush, Georgie Britton, Caroline Skinner, Denise Paul, and Ed Casey at BBC Worldwide for their invaluable assistance.

IDW founded by Ted Adams, Alex Garner, Kris Oprisko, and Robbie Robbins | International Rights Representative, Christine Meyer: christine@gfloystudio.com

ISBN: 978-1-61377-155-6

15 14 13 12 1 2 3 4

Ted Adams, CEO & Publisher
Greg Goldstein, President & COO
Robbie Robbins, EVP/Sr. Graphic Artist
Chris Ryall, Chief Creative Officer/Editor-in-Chief
Matthew Ruzicka, CPA, Chief Financial Officer
Alan Payne, VP of Sales

Become our fan on Facebook **facebook.com/idwpublishing**
Follow us on Twitter **@idwpublishing**
Check us out on YouTube **youtube.com/idwpublishing**
www.IDWPUBLISHING.com

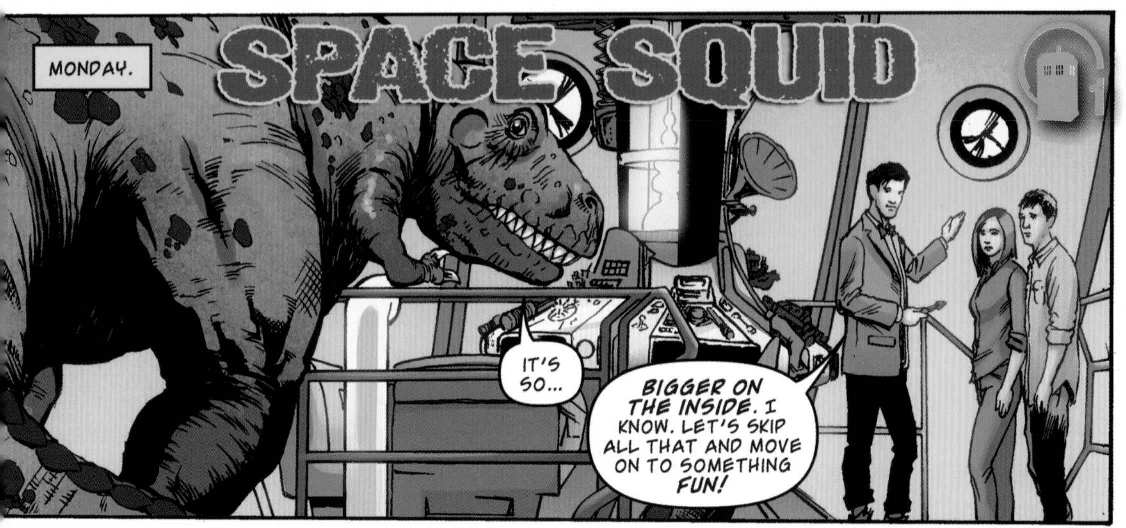
MONDAY.
SPACE SQUID
IT'S SO...
BIGGER ON THE INSIDE. I KNOW. LET'S SKIP ALL THAT AND MOVE ON TO SOMETHING *FUN!*

...ACTUALLY, I WAS GOING TO SAY '*CLAUSTROPHOBIC*'.

COME ON, KEVIN, LET'S FIND YOU A ROOM.
A *LARGE* ROOM.

YEAH... MIGHT NEED SOME *HELP* HERE.
IS THERE A *FREIGHT LIFT* IN THE TARDIS, DOCTOR?

TUESDAY.
COME ON, KEVIN, GET IN! SITTING BULL AND HIS MEN ARE COMING!
I KNOW! THEY JUST HIT ME WITH AN ARROW!
I MIGHT BE A ROBOT, BUT I HAVE PAIN RECEPTORS! OW!
POLICE PUBLIC CALL BOX

WEDNESDAY.
I'M LIEUTENANT ADDISON OF THE L.A.P.D.—THIS IS MY PARTNER, LIEUTENANT...
...KEVIN.
JUST THE FACTS, MA'AM.

ROOAAARRRR!
YOU KNOW, I KINDA MISS THE RUNNING AWAY LOTS PART.
THURSDAY.

LATER THURSDAY.
PULL THE EGG WHISK! PULL THE EGG WHISK!
HOW?! I CAN'T REACH IT! HAVE YOU SEEN THE ARMS I HAVE?

FRIDAY.
ARE YOU ALL RIGHT, KEVIN?
OH, HELLO, RORY.
NO, NOT REALLY.

I ALWAYS WANTED TO SEE HE WORLD, EXPERIENCE NEW, WELL... EXPERIENCES.
I KNEW THAT I WAS MORE THAN JUST A DINOSAUR. BUT I'M NOT, AM I?

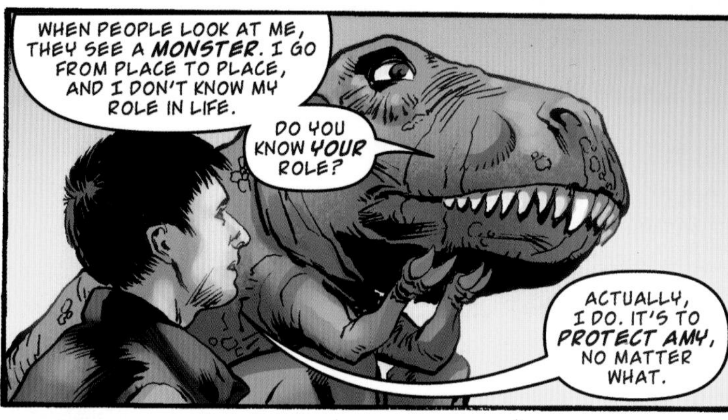
WHEN PEOPLE LOOK AT ME, THEY SEE A MONSTER. I GO FROM PLACE TO PLACE, AND I DON'T KNOW MY ROLE IN LIFE.
DO YOU KNOW YOUR ROLE?
ACTUALLY, I DO. IT'S TO PROTECT AMY, NO MATTER WHAT.

SOMETIMES I USED TO FEEL LIKE I DIDN'T FIT IN HERE, BUT YOU KNOW WHAT? THAT'S FINE WITH ME.
BECAUSE IT'S EASIER TO LOOK AFTER SOMEONE WHEN EVERYONE OVERLOOKS YOU.
BUT FOR 2000 YEARS I KEPT HER SAFE, AND I'M NOT GOING TO STOP NOW.

YOU'LL FIND YOUR REASON TO CONTINUE, KEVIN. IT MIGHT NOT BE TODAY, OR EVEN TOMORROW...
...BUT IT'S OUT THERE. AND WHEN YOU DO FIND IT...

'...YOU'LL KNOW IT'S YOUR DESTINY'!
TOMORROW. SPACE STATION E11—NEBULA BASE.

COMMANDER KATIC! MA'AM!
WHAT IS IT, FILLION?

MORE OF THESE ZEALOTS ARRIVED ON THE LAST CREW SHIP!
THEY CALL THEMSELVES THE ACOLYTES OF THE HOLY SPACE SQUID!
YEAH, I'VE HEARD. THEY RECKON THE END OF THE UNIVERSE STARTS HERE, RIGHT? WITH A GIANT OCTOPUS OR SOMETHING?
KEEP THEM LOCKED DOWN UNTIL WE CAN SHIP THEM ALL BACK TO WHATEVER ASYLUM THEY ESCAPED FROM.

THIS STATION ALREADY HAS ENOUGH 'LEGENDS ABOUT IT...
...LET'S NOT ADD ANOTHER!

BOW DOWN BEFORE THE HOLY SPACE SQUID!
THE END OF DAYS IS COMING!

BOW DOWN BEFORE THE HOLY SPACE SQUID!
THE END OF DAYS IS COMING!
ARE THEY STILL CHANTING, MAJOR? I THOUGHT THEY WOULD HAVE GIVEN UP BY NOW.
NO, MA'AM. IF ANYTHING, THEY'RE GETTING WORSE.
APPARENTLY, SOME HIGH-RANKING PRIEST IS ARRIVING TODAY. GONNA GUIDE THEM PERSONALLY THROUGH THE SQUID RAPTURE.

IT SEEMS THAT THE END OF THE WORLD IS TODAY AT 1700 HOURS. OR SOMETHING LIKE THAT.
THE SQUID WILL EMBRACE THE FAITHFUL WITHIN ITS HOLY TENTACLES.

REALLY? I MIGHT HAVE TO HAVE A WORD WITH THESE ACOLYTES. SEE IF THEY WANT TO GIVE THIS UNBELIEVER HERE THEIR POSSESSIONS BEFORE THEY GO.
AFTER ALL, THEY WON'T NEED THEM, AND THERE ARE A COUPLE OF CHOICE SPACE YACHTS OUT THERE READY FOR THE TAKING.

VWORP
VWORP

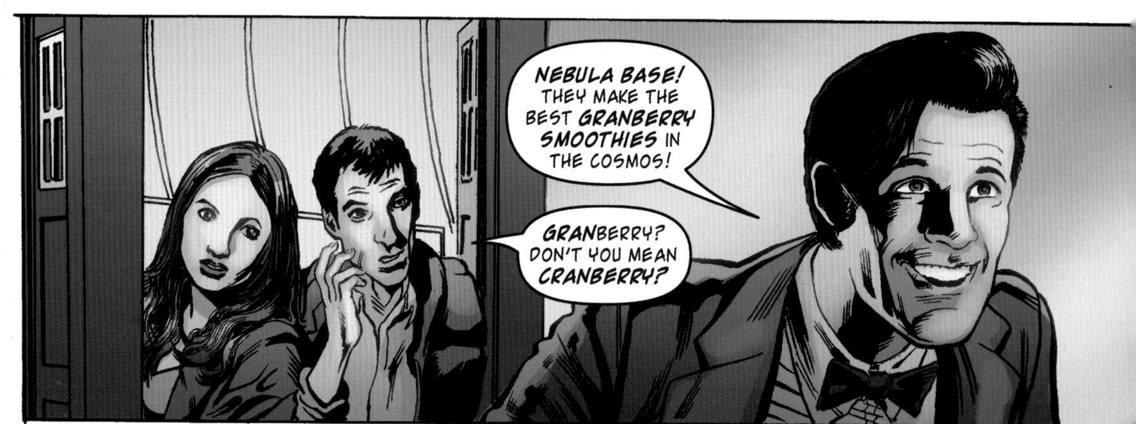

NEBULA BASE! THEY MAKE THE BEST GRANBERRY SMOOTHIES IN THE COSMOS!
GRANBERRY? DON'T YOU MEAN CRANBERRY?

GRANBERRY. STARTS WITH A 'G'. LARGE THING, SPIKY ENDS. TASTES LIKE MINCE.
NEBULA BASE IS PERCHED ON THE EDGE OF A RADION SINGULARITY. THE SOLAR RADIATION BRINGS OUT THE FLAVOUR, YOU SEE.

MINCE, EH? YUM YUM. A MINCE SMOOTHIE.
I'M STILL ASLEEP, AREN'T I? IT'S A BAD DREAM, AND I'M STILL ASLEEP.
IF YOU DON'T STOP WHINING, I'LL PUSH YOU OUT OF YOUR BUNK. THEN YOU'LL WAKE UP.

UM, DOCTOR? DO YOU THINK I SHOULD COME WITH YOU?
AFTER THAT... MISUNDERSTANDING IN JAPAN?
PURELY A CULTURAL THING, KEVIN. THEY THOUGHT YOU WERE GOING TO EAT TOKYO.
STAY HERE. WE'LL PICK UP A DRINK AND THEN BE BACK IN A FLASH.

POLICE PUBLIC CALL BOX
YEAH. BECAUSE THAT ALWAYS HAPPENS.

COMMANDER KATIC! MAJOR FILLION! WE HAVE AN INCOMING TRANSMISSION!
THE STAR CRUISER 'HEAVEN'S TENTACLE' IS REQUESTING PERMISSION TO DOCK!
THAT'LL BE OUR HIGH PRIEST ARRIVING, THEN.
LET THEM IN, LT. HUERTAS. TELL THEM THEY'VE GOT A BIT OF A WELCOME COMMITTEE, THOUGH.

HEAVEN'S TENTACLE, YOU ARE WELCOME TO DOCK AT BAY 17.
APPRECIATED, NEBULA BASE.

CAPTAIN, WE JUST NOTICED A PROJECTILE LAUNCHED FROM YOUR SHIP. CAN YOU EXPLAIN?
IT'S NOTHING, COMMANDER. OUR PASSENGER WANTED TO RELEASE SOME HOLY RELICS INTO THE VACUUM.
TO WELCOME SOME GOD, OR SOMETHING. NOTHING MORE.

OKAY, CAPTAIN. PREPARE FOR DOCKING COORDINATES—
COMMANDER! THE PROMENADE IS HEATING UP! THE ACOLYTES HAVE SEEN THE SHIP!
WE NEED MORE MEN ON THE GROUND!

THEY'LL ONLY GET WORSE WHEN HE ARRIVES. BREAK OUT THE BIG DAWG, PETTY OFFICER DEVER.
LET'S SEE HOW THEY LIKE HIM.

THE NATIVES ARE GETTING RESTLESS, DOCTOR. WE NEED TO GET OUT OF HERE!
BUT I HAVEN'T GOT MY GRANBERRY SMOOTHIE YET—
I'LL COOK YOU A SPAG BOL! COME ON!

FOR THE SPACE SQUID!
NO BLASTERS! NO BLASTERS!

COME ON... WHERE ARE YOU?

DON'T MESS WITH BIG DAWG!
BIG DAWG—

—EXPLODES.
HMMMMMM

FOOM
SECURITY TO COMMAND! SONIC WEAPONS! BIG DAWG'S DOWN!

AND I THINK I'M NEXT—

ROOAAARR

THAT'S A NEW ADDITION TO THE SECURITY TEAM.
LOOK! UP ON THE GANTRY! IT'S THE HIGH PRIEST!

ACOLYTES OF THE SPACE SQUID! THIS WILL NOT DO!
WE ARE HERE TO SPREAD LOVE AND TENTACLES, NOT HATE AND VIOLENCE! STOP THIS NOW!

YOU KEEP TALKING OF THIS SPACE SQUID, BUT WHERE IS IT? EH?
HOKEY RELIGIONS AND MAGIC CEPHALOPODS ARE NO SUBSTITUTE FOR A GOOD BLASTER AT YOUR SIDE!

TRUE. I SHOULD, AS THEY SAY, 'PUT MY MONEY WHERE MY MOUTH IS'.
VERY WELL. REJOICE, MY BRETHREN...

...FOR THE TIME OF THE SPACE SQUID IS AT HAND!
COME! COME TO THE MAIN HANGAR!

COME! QUICK! BEFORE SECURITY CATCHES YOU!
WHY? IS THERE ANYTHING WE'VE DONE THAT WOULD MAKE SECURITY WANT TO CATCH US?

THERE! THAT MAN! SONIC WEAPON!

DOCTOR!

BETA TEAM, RIGHT? I SAW THE OTHER MAN'S SONIC DEVICE!
GOING THAT CLOSE? BALLSY! I LIKE IT!
THAT'S US... BALLSY... I SUPPOSE...
LOOK, COULD WE JUST STOP FOR A MINUTE AND GET OUR FRIEND?

WHY BOTHER? SURELY HE'S RIGHT WHERE HE WANTS TO BE!
AND THE UNIVERSE ENDS IN AN HOUR OR TWO, ANYWAY!

ENSIGN QUINN, GET THIS MAN WHATEVER HE NEEDS.
WHAT I NEED IS TO SEE THE FOOTAGE OF THE SHIP AS IT ARRIVED.
AWFULLY CONVENIENT FOR SOME ALL-POWERFUL SQUID GOD TO ARRIVE JUST AS HE DOES, ISN'T IT?

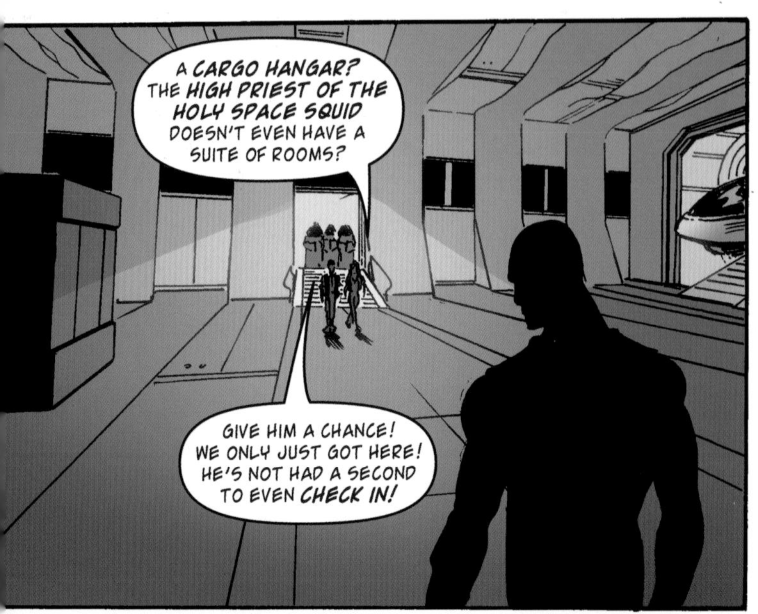
A CARGO HANGAR? THE HIGH PRIEST OF THE HOLY SPACE SQUID DOESN'T EVEN HAVE A SUITE OF ROOMS?
GIVE HIM A CHANCE! WE ONLY JUST GOT HERE! HE'S NOT HAD A SECOND TO EVEN CHECK IN!

AND THERE ARE MORE IMPORTANT THINGS TO DO THAN CHECK IN, YOUNG WOMAN.
LIKE PERSONALLY THANK TWO OF MY FINEST ACOLYTES.

WHAT, US?
I MEAN, YES, US!
I WILL ADMIT I DIDN'T REALISE THAT WE HAD ANY BACKUP AGENTS OUT THERE. JONES IS MY FINEST.
I APOLOGISE THAT HE GOT TO THE TARGET FIRST.

OH, NOT A PROBLEM, WE UNDERSTAND FULLY. LEFT HAND KNOWING RIGHT HAND AND ALL THAT.
WHY ONLY TAKE OUT THE ROBOT? WHY NOT THE GUARDS, TOO?

BECAUSE WE ONLY WANTED THE NON-HUMAN CREW DISABLED.
THE 'BIG DAWG', AS THEY LIKE TO CALL HIM, IS... WAS THE ONLY NON-HUMAN SECURITY ON THE STATION.

WITH IT GONE, THERE IS NOBODY LEFT TO STOP US AFTER THE MIND CONTROL BEGINS.
WHICH IS IN ABOUT... OH, NOW.

IT'S A COLEOIDEAN. NASTY LITTLE SQUIDDY THING. LIKES TO SUCK BRAINS.
USUALLY ABOUT FIVE FEET TALL.
WELL, I THINK WE CAN SAFELY SAY THAT THIS ONE IS A DAMN SIGHT MORE THAN FIVE FEET, DOCTOR!
ANY GENIUS IDEAS INVOLVING THAT?

ACTUALLY, YES. THIS SINGULARITY THAT YOU'RE BESIDE SPEWS OUT RADION RADIATION. GREAT FOR SMOOTHIES, ALSO FOR SQUIDS.
THINK OF THOSE SPONGES THAT ARE TINY AND GROW WHEN YOU STICK THEM IN WATER. NO? DON'T HAVE THOSE ANYMORE?

NOW, CHANGE THE WORDS SPONGE AND WATER WITH SQUID AND RADION NEBULA.
AND HE'S STILL GROWING. WE NEED TO STOP IT.

COLEOIDEANS LOVE TO SUCK BRAINS, BUT THEY LOVE TO CONTROL THEM FIRST. NORMAL SIZE? IT MIGHT BE ABLE TO MANAGE THREE, FOUR PEOPLE.
THIS SIZE? THE WHOLE SPACE STATION IS A BREEZE.
SO, WHAT DO WE NEED TO DO THEN? BLOW IT UP? WE'RE NOT A MILITARY STATION!

THAT'S NICE, BECAUSE I DON'T LIKE GUNS. WE'LL NEED TO REVERSE THE RADION.
DOES YOUR MEDICAL BAY HAVE QUANTITIES OF THE BURN REDUCER STELLION XT? I COULD KNOCK SOMETHING UP WITH THAT AND SOME TOOTHPASTE.
THAT SHOULDN'T BE A PROBLEM, DOCTOR. I'LL HAVE QUINN ESCORT YOU TO THE MEDICAL BAY.

MEGA!
HMM. DO WE SAY MEGA NOW? REALLY?
I DON'T THINK WE DO. IGNORE THAT. INSERT A HAPPY PHRASE OF YOUR OWN INSTEAD.

WHILE I DO THIS, IT'S VERY IMPORTANT THAT YOU FIND MY TWO FRIENDS.
THEY'RE PROBABLY IN TROUBLE AND DOING SOMETHING THAT'LL PUSH THEM FURTHER INTO IT.
WILL DO, DOCTOR. I'LL JUST PROVIDE—

—NNNG— ARRGHHH! THE SPACE SQUID!

AH. THIS ISN'T GOOD.
SSSSSPACE SSSSSQUIDDD...

DOCTOR! THEY LET ME GO FREE, BUT NOW EVERYONE'S FALLING TO THE FLOOR AND CLUTCHING THEIR HEADS!
WHAT DO WE DO?
YES... I WAS HOPING THAT WOULDN'T HAPPEN RIGHT AWAY...

SERVE THE HOLY SPACE SQUID.
DIE FOR THE HOLY SPACE SQUID.

RUN, KEVIN!

THE HOLY SPACE SQUID HAS **SPOKEN!** HIS WISHES MUST BE MADE FLESH!
WE MUST DESTROY THIS BASE AND THIS **NEBULA** IN HIS NAME!

ONLY **THEN** WILL WE BE ABLE TO ASCEND TO THE **SQUID HEAVEN!**
SQUID...

QUICK, KEVIN! HELP ME BAR THE DOOR!
TWO OF OUR MOST **TRUSTED ACOLYTES** WILL UNDERTAKE THIS TASK...
...GIVE THE **DETONATION** DEVICE TO THE **HONOURED MARTYRS!**

TAKE THIS AS AN **APOLOGY** FOR NOT ALLOWING YOU TO DESTROY THE ROBOT.
I GIVE YOU SOMETHING TO RAISE YOU FAR **HIGHER** IN THE SPACE SQUID'S EYES!
YOU HONOUR US.

AMY! RORY! AMY! RORY!

WHAT? NO!
HOW COULD I BE SO STUPID?! THEY'RE ONLY HUMAN, OF COURSE THEY'D BE CONTROLLED!

THE SPACE SQUID IS GOING TO BLOW US UP? HOW DO WE STOP THIS?
WELL, ACTUALLY, IT RATHER LOOKS LIKE AMY AND RORY ARE GOING TO BLOW US UP. BETTER WORK OUT A PLAN.
DO YOU HAVE ONE? AH. PITY.
MICROPHONE! WE NEED A MICROPHONE!

ATTENTION, ALL SQUID-LOVING ZEALOTS!
THIS BASE ISN'T QUITE AS CONTROLLED AS YOU BELIEVED IT WAS!

HOW CAN THIS BE? NOBODY IS LEFT UNSAVED! WHO IS THIS?
WELL, EVERY PLAN HAS ITS FLAWS, YOU KNOW! I MEAN, I'M HERE, AND KEVIN'S HERE... SAY HELLO, KEVIN.
HELLO.
AND I THINK WE NEED TO HAVE A CHAT BEFORE YOU GO ABOUT DESTROYING EVERYTHING.

YOU SEE, AS FOR WHO I AM? I'M THE ANTI-SQUID.
AND I WANT TO PARLAY THE GROUND RULES FOR ARMAGEDDON. ONE HOUR, THE CONTROL ROOM?
BRING ALL YOUR FRIENDS. OH, AND YOUR BOMB.

HI-YO, KEVIN! AWAY!

ARE YOU SURE THIS WILL WORK?
YOU'RE A ROBOT, KEVIN, BUT YOUR PROBLEM IS THAT YOU HAVE DINOSAUR ARMS. TINY.
AND NO JETPACK. JETPACKS ARE COOL. AND SURPRISINGLY NEEDED RIGHT NOW.

HERE, PUT IT ON, SEE WHAT IT LOOKS LIKE.

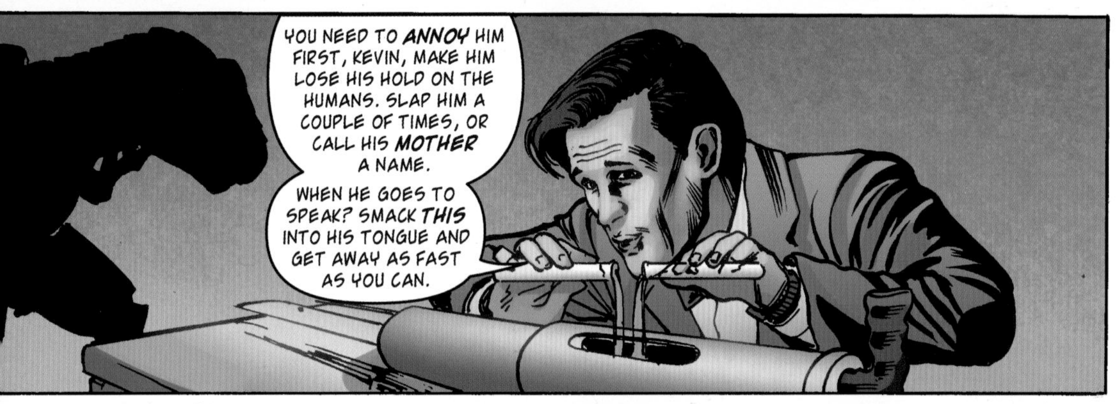
YOU NEED TO ANNOY HIM FIRST, KEVIN, MAKE HIM LOSE HIS HOLD ON THE HUMANS. SLAP HIM A COUPLE OF TIMES, OR CALL HIS MOTHER A NAME.
WHEN HE GOES TO SPEAK? SMACK THIS INTO HIS TONGUE AND GET AWAY AS FAST AS YOU CAN.

SO, ARE WE READY FOR THIS? SHOES SHINED AND RARING TO—
—OH, KEVIN. YOU LOOK SO COOL.

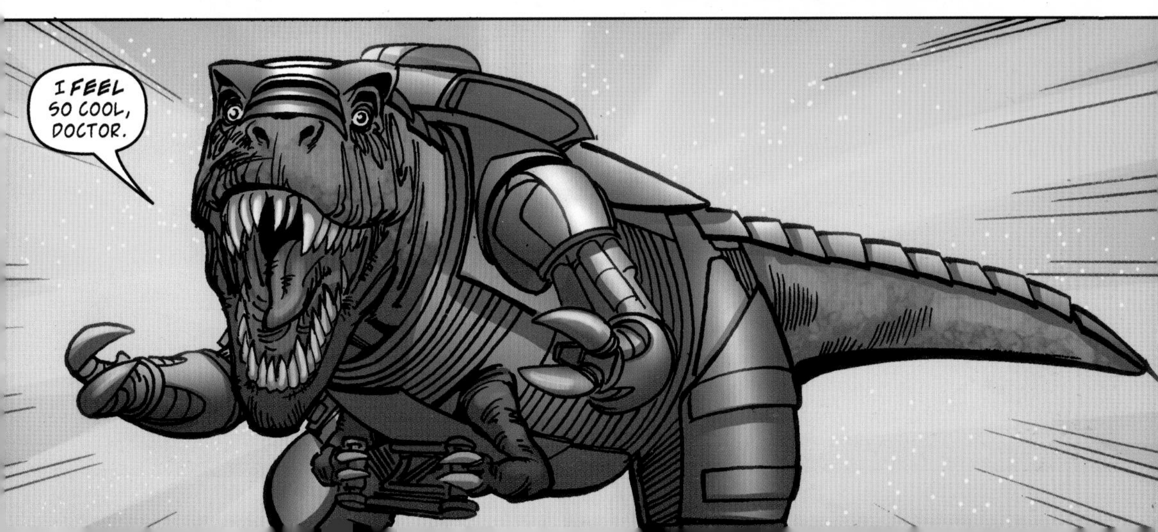
I FEEL SO COOL, DOCTOR.

TELL US ABOUT THE ANTI-SQUID, RORY. IS HE A BRAVE MAN? A CLEVER ONE?
WHY DON'T YOU ASK HIM YOURSELF...

...AS HE'S STANDING RIGHT HERE.

SO, HOW LONG HAVE YOU BEEN CONTROLLED BY THE COLEOIDEAN?
YOU DON'T HAVE THE EYES-ROLLED-BACK LOOK OF THE OTHERS, SO I'M GUESSING FOR QUITE A WHILE.
HERETIC! I AM NOT CONTROLLED BY IT! I WORSHIP IT!

OF COURSE YOU DO. EVERY DAY SINCE IT TOLD YOU TO.
AH, RORY POND. I EXPECTED MORE OF YOU. SICK OF BEING A FREE MAN, ARE YOU?

AND YOU, AMELIA JESSICA POND. YOU WHO BROKE THE DREAM LORD'S GAME...
...BEATEN BY A NOT-QUITE-FRIED CALAMARI. I SHOULD TAKE YOU BACK TO LEADWORTH. IN SHAME.

NNUHH... DIED... TURNED INTO A ROMAN... VERY DISTRACTING...
FISH FINGERS... CUSTARD... RAGGEDY DOCTOR...

HOW IS THIS POSSIBLE?! THEIR MINDS ARE CONTROLLED!
JUST BECAUSE YOU CONTROL A MIND, DOESN'T MEAN YOU OWN IT.
THE HOST WILL ALWAYS REASSERT.

YOU THINK YOU CAN CONFUSE HIM? HALT HIM?
DELAY THE USE OF THE BOMB? I'LL DO IT MYSELF–
UH-UH, HIGH PRIEST. I DON'T THINK SO.

AMY! RORY! YOU'RE BACK! JUST IN TIME FOR THE CABARET!
WHAT HAPPENED?
AND WHAT AM I HOLDING?
IT'S A BOMB, ISN'T IT? I'M HOLDING A BOMB.

THREE OF YOU AGAINST A SPACE STATION? DON'T MAKE ME LAUGH!
IT'S FOUR, ACTUALLY. DON'T YOU REMEMBER KEVIN? I MADE HIM SAY HELLO AND EVERYTHING!

YOUR BOSS OUT THERE NEEDS TO CONCENTRATE ON ALL OF YOU TO KEEP YOU CONTROLLED.
THE FACT THAT AMY AND RORY ARE FREE SHOWS THAT HE'S OVERSTRETCHED HIS RESOURCES. HE CAN'T HAVE ANY DISTRACTIONS.

"CAN YOU GUESS WHAT KEVIN'S ABOUT TO DO?"
DAAN DAN DUHN DUHN DAH-DAH DUHN...
HEY, SQUIDDY...

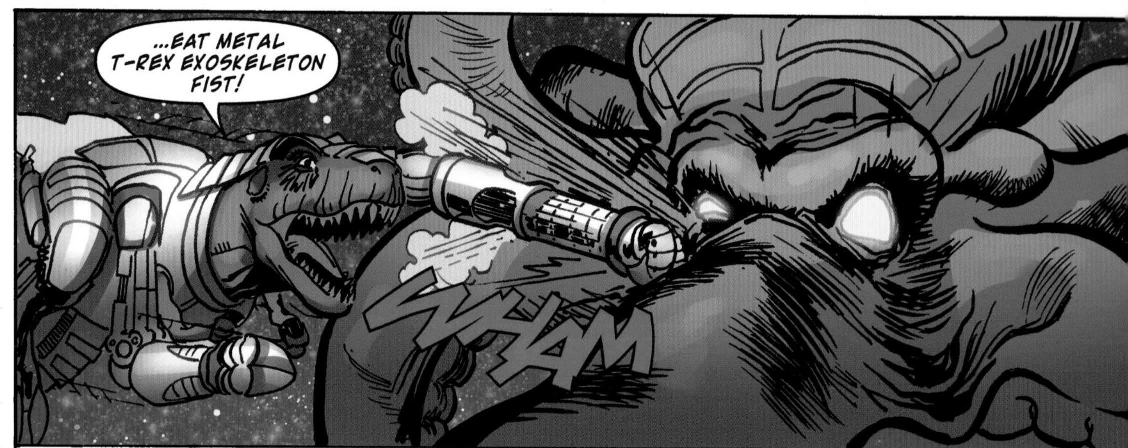
...EAT METAL T-REX EXOSKELETON FIST!
WHAM

DID HE JUST SAY WHAT I THINK HE SAID? AND DID I HEAR SINGING?
EARLY DAYS. HE'S IMPROVISING. YOU KNOW WHAT ACTORS CAN BE LIKE.

ARGH! GET OFF ME!

AAIIEEEEEEEE
FOOOSHHHH

NOW, KEVIN! WHILE IT SCREAMS!
WHAT'S HAPPENING?! MY HEAD!

I'M TERRIBLY SORRY ABOUT THIS, BUT YOU DO RATHER SEEM TO WANT TO DESTROY EVERYTHING!

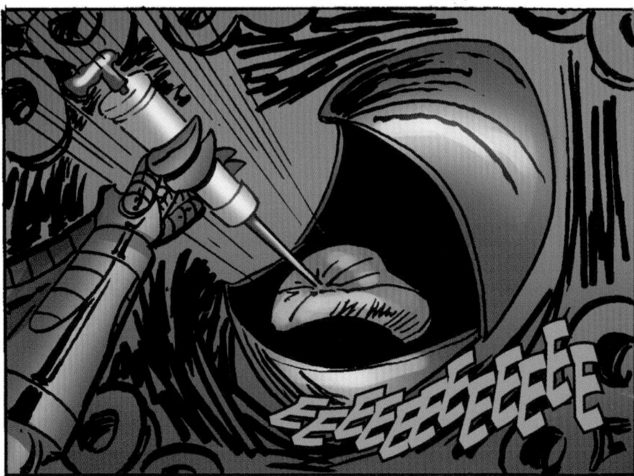
EEEEEEEEEEEEE

COVER YOUR EARS—

KRA-KOOM

IT'S DONE, DOCTOR. THE SQUID... IT'S UNCONSCIOUS...

...I'M BRINGING IT IN.

LATER.
FIFTEEN YEARS IT CONTROLLED ME. THANK YOU FOR FREEING ME FROM ITS GRASP!
WHAT WILL YOU DO NOW?

WELL, COMMANDER KATIC SAID I COULD KEEP THE CHURCH GOING. IT APPARENTLY MAKES THE STATION A SMALL PROFIT.
AND I DON'T REALLY KNOW ANYTHING ELSE!

IT'S A TOURIST THING. HEAD OFFICE LIKES THE IDEA OF THIS BEING THE LAST SIGHTING OF THE HOLY SPACE SQUID AND ALL THAT.
PEOPLE WILL FLOCK TO VISIT IT WHILE THE REAL THING IS SHIPPED FAR AWAY.

WILL YOU BE ABLE TO KEEP THE ACOLYTES UNDER CONTROL? I MEAN, THEY'RE A ROWDY LOT—
OH, I THINK OUR NEW SECURITY OFFICER CAN KEEP THEM UNDER CONTROL.

UM. YES. HELLO, DOCTOR.
IF IT'S OKAY WITH YOU, I THINK I'M GOING TO STAY. I'VE FOUND A PURPOSE HERE.

OF COURSE IT'S OKAY! THE WHOLE POINT OF TRAVELLING IS TO FIND A PLACE YOU WANT TO CALL HOME!

GOOD LUCK, KEVIN. WE'LL COME AND VISIT.
THANK YOU FOR YOUR ADVICE, RORY. MAKE SURE YOU KEEP TAKING IT, TOO.
SO, WE TRAVEL UNTIL WE FIND A HOME, EH, DOCTOR?
SO, WHERE'S YOURS?

POLICE PUBLIC CALL BOX
OH, MINE FOUND ME BEFORE I EVEN STARTED TRAVELLING...
...AND SHE'S LOOKED AFTER ME EVER SINCE.
COME ON, PONDS. UNIVERSE WON'T BE KEPT WAITING AND ALL THAT. I HAVE THE GREATEST SLUSHIE IN THE COSMOS TO SHOW YOU!
VWORP VWORP
THE END.

THE 45TH CENTURY.
BODY SNATCHED
2
AHA! THE TRANS-UNIVERSAL UNION! ANY LETTER, ANY TIME, ANY COSMOS!
A POST OFFICE. YOU'VE BROUGHT US TO A POST OFFICE.
OF COURSE! HOW ELSE CAN I PICK UP MY MAIL?
YOU GET MAIL? I THOUGHT YOU GET CALLS ON THAT MAGIC PHONE THING OF YOURS.
TRUE, BUT I NEED ALTERNATE WAYS TO GET MESSAGES THROUGH TO ME FROM MY FRIENDS.
THE GREAT THING ABOUT THIS PLACE IS THAT ALL MAIL IS PLACED INTO A STASIS DRAWER. YOU CAN COME BACK HUNDREDS OF YEARS LATER AND IT'S STILL WAITING FOR YOU!
RIGHT. SO, HOW LONG AGO DID YOU SET THIS UP?
I HAVEN'T, YET.

HE HASN'T SET THIS UP YET. SO, OF COURSE, IT'LL BE WAITING FOR HIM. BECAUSE HE'S THE DOCTOR. NORMALITY IS JUST A WORD HE'S HEARD OF.
YOU WANT NORMAL? HAVE YOU SEEN HOW WE LIVE LATELY?
FAIR POINT.
SO, HOW DOES THIS WORK THEN?
WELL, THE NEXT TIME I DROP YOU TWO OFF FOR A BREAK, I'LL GO BACK AND SET UP THE ACCOUNT, THEN PASS THE DETAILS TO THE PEOPLE WHO NEED THEM.
THEN, A FEW HUNDRED YEARS LATER, I'LL COME BACK AND PICK UP THE MAIL. NO, WAIT, ALREADY DONE THAT PART.
'HEY, DOC, WANNA MAKE SOME MOOLAH? WE'VE FOUND A DIAMOND PLANET.' I REALLY SHOULDN'T HAVE GIVEN HIM THIS ADDRESS.
OH! A LETTER FROM THE HORSE LORD OF KHAN!
YOU KNOW SOMEONE CALLED THE HORSE LORD OF KHAN? THAT'S HIS NAME? MUST HAVE BEEN A LONG CHRISTENING.
MAYBE HIS TRUE NAME IS A SERIES OF SNORTS AND WHINNIES?
HE LIKES TO BE CALLED TREVOR, ACTUALLY. HMM. HE'S IN TROUBLE. HE NEEDS OUR HELP.
THE LETTER WAS SENT TWO HUNDRED YEARS AGO—
TWO HUNDRED YEARS? HOW DOES THAT HELP? OH. YEAH, I GET IT. TIME MACHINE. OF COURSE.
I'LL JUST SHUT UP NOW.

HE DOESN'T SAY MUCH. PROBABLY COULDN'T WRITE IT ALL DOWN, BUT HE'S CURRENTLY LOCKED DOWN IN BEDLAM.
BEDLAM? THE INSANE ASYLUM?
BUT THE BETHLEHEM ROYAL PSYCHIATRIC HOSPITAL IS IN VICTORIAN LONDON! TELL ME WE'RE NOT GOING BACK THERE AGAIN?
NOT THAT BEDLAM, RORY, BUT SIMILAR. TOO SIMILAR.
THE PLANET OF BEDLAM, MODELED ON THE ORIGINAL HOSPITAL.
WELL, MORE OF AN ASTEROID IN A GEOSTATIONARY ORBIT AROUND A PLANET THAN A PLANET, PER SE.
STILL, A CALL FOR HELP IS A CALL FOR HELP. HE'D DO THE SAME FOR ME.
ALTHOUGH HE'D PROBABLY, YOU KNOW, USE HORSES OR SOMETHING.
HOLD ON!
VWORP VWORP

THE PLANET HOSPITAL OF BEDLAM. A LARGE HOSPITAL WITH ONLY ONE TYPE OF PATIENT.
BIOGROWERS.
BIOGROWERS?
OR GREEN SUITS, OR GROWBOYS, PLUG AND PLAYS OR PETRI PEOPLE. THE NAMES THAT HUMANS COME UP WITH FOR THEM ARE ENDLESS.
IT SAYS HERE THEIR OFFICIAL NAME IS BIO-ORGANIC PLASMATOID CREATION, BUT THEY PRETTY MUCH MEAN INTELLIGENT BROCCOLI.
CREATED TWO CENTURIES EARLIER, THE BIOGROWERS ARE THE PERFECT SERVANT. GROWN FROM POD TO PERSON IN A WEEK, THEY LIVE FOR A HUNDRED YEARS, NEVER AGING.
ALWAYS FOLLOWING ORDERS WITHOUT THE INTELLIGENCE TO QUESTION THEM, ABLE TO PERFORM LIMITED MANUAL TASKS.
SO, WHAT'S WRONG WITH THE ONES HERE? THEY DON'T EVEN SEEM TO KNOW THAT WE'RE BESIDE THEM!
THEY DON'T. IT SAYS HERE THAT BIOGROWERS HAVE ONE MAJOR FLAW. A BODY THAT LASTS A HUNDRED YEARS...
...BUT A BRAIN THAT ONLY LASTS FIFTY. THE SECOND HALF OF, WELL, THEIR LIVES IS LIVED IN A CATATONIC STATE.
PROBLEM IS, THOUSANDS OF CATATONIC BIOGROWERS MEAN A MASSIVE DRAIN OF RESOURCES. SO BEDLAM WAS BUILT.
A PLACE TO DUMP YOUR SERVANT WHEN HE BREAKS DOWN, TENDED TO BY OTHERS, LIKE THIS ONE.
STATE YOUR PURPOSE.
SEE? THEY MANAGE SIMPLE SENTENCES, BUT THE BROCHURE SAYS THAT'S ABOUT ALL.

WELL, FOR A START, THE BROCHURE WAS WRITTEN BY IDIOTS. IF YOU DON'T HAVE AN APPOINTMENT, I THINK YOU SHOULD COME WITH ME.
DR. RUBIN TAKES A VERY DIM VIEW OF INTERLOPERS, I'LL TELL YOU NOW.
I MIGHT BE WRONG, BUT HE DOESN'T SEEM UNINTELLIGENT.
I KNOW! FASCINATING, ISN'T IT? IT SAYS HERE THAT BIOGROWERS CAN'T HAVE CONVERSATIONS, LET ALONE REASON!
SO, HOW DOES THIS ONE MANAGE IT?
SORRY TO BOTHER YOU, SIR, BUT I FOUND THESE THREE PEOPLE SKULKING AROUND IN THE PLAY ROOM.
VISITORS? WE WEREN'T SCHEDULED ANY VISITORS. WE NEVER HAVE VISITORS!
SEE THIS? YES, WE'RE FROM HERE. AND THIS IS A SURPRISE AUDIT. FROM THE PEOPLE YOU SEE HERE.
WE WANT FULL ACCESS AND EXPLANATIONS, DR. RUBIN.
I'M THE DOCTOR. THESE ARE MY ASSISTANTS, AMY AND NURSE POND.
WILLIAMS.
POND. HE'LL BE EXAMINING THE BIOGROWERS.
I WILL? I WILL.
OF COURSE! HOW EXCITING! HOMEWORLD HAVE NEVER SENT AN AUDIT BEFORE!
NURSE HELLA! HELP NURSE POND WITH ANYTHING HE NEEDS.
YES, DR. RUBIN.
COME WITH ME, PLEASE.
GO WITH THEM, AMY, YOU KNOW WHAT TO LOOK OUT FOR.
SO, DR. RUBIN, TELL ME ABOUT YOUR WORK HERE!

SO, HOW LONG HAVE YOU BEEN HERE?
ABOUT TWO YEARS. AND THAT'S TWO YEARS TOO LONG.
YOU DON'T LIKE IT HERE?
NOBODY LIKES IT HERE! IT'S A HOUSE OF THE DEAD—THEY JUST HAVEN'T STOPPED MOVING YET.
I'M A NURSE. I TEND TO THE SICK. BUT THERE'S NOTHING HERE TO TEND—THE GREEN SUITS JUST WAIT UNTIL THEIR CLOCK RUNS OUT.
ONCE THE MIND GOES... NOTHING.
HERE, LOOK FOR YOURSELVES.

SO, WHAT HAPPENS?
DESIGN FLAW. IN THEIR 51ST YEAR OF LIFE, THE BRAIN SIMPLY SWITCHES OFF.
THINK OF IT LIKE A COMPUTER—THE BODY IS THE CASE, THE MIND THE DRIVE THAT RUNS IT.
AFTER FIFTY YEARS THE DRIVE IS WIPED OF ALL DATA. THE COMPUTER STILL LOOKS FINE, BUT IT'S EMPTY OF ALL INFORMATION AND COMMANDS.
SO, THEY HAVE NO USE? THAT'S HARSH.
WELL, THAT'S NOT TOTALLY TRUE. DR. RUBIN HAS COME UP WITH AN INSPIRED SOLUTION—TRANSMIGRATORY MEMORY MAPPING.
BASICALLY, HE BELIEVES THAT ONE DAY WE COULD PUT SOMEONE ELSE'S MIND INTO A BIOGROWER BODY.
THINK OF THE POSSIBILITIES! YOU'RE PARALYSED, OR HAVE A DEBILITATING, TERMINAL DISEASE? NOT ANYMORE!
YOU'RE THE GREATEST MIND IN THE UNIVERSE AND YOU'RE DYING—TRANSFER TO A NEW BODY! FIFTY GUARANTEED YEARS OF HEALTH!
AND THE BIOGROWERS DON'T MIND THIS?
WELL, THIS IS ALL STILL THEORETICAL—WE'RE YEARS AWAY FROM TESTING!

WHAT'S DOWN THERE?
NOTHING. THAT'S THE INTENSIVE CARE UNIT. SOMETIMES A TEST REACTS BADLY.
THEY'RE KEPT AWAY FROM THE OTHERS, AND DR. RUBIN TENDS TO THEM PERSONALLY.
ARE YOU THINKING WHAT I'M THINKING?
IT'D BETTER NOT BE ANYTHING ABOUT THE PRETTY YOUNG NURSE BESIDE YOU.
KEEP HER DISTRACTED, BUT NOT TOO DISTRACTED. I'LL GO AND HAVE A LOOK, SEE IF TREVOR IS DOWN THERE.
IT'S BROCCOLI. NOTHING MORE THAN BROCCOLI.
HOW BAD CAN AN EXPERIMENT ON BROCCOLI GO?
CLICK
WHERE ARE MY LEGS?! I SHOULD HAVE SEVEN! WHERE ARE THE OTHER FIVE?
YOU THINK YOU ARE BETTER THAN ME? THE RE'NAR ARE THE FIERCEST IN THE COSMOS!
PAH! MY CHILDREN COULD BEAT YOU, LIZARD SCUM!

OH MY GOD... THIS CAN'T BE HAPPENING!
ARGH!
PLEASE! I HAVE A REFLECTION! WHY DO I HAVE A REFLECTION?! I CAN'T TURN THE FILTER OFF!
I CAN'T BECOME SATURNYNIAN ANYMORE!
BACK AWAY, VAMPYRIC SCUM! GO STAND IN THE SUN!
NOT THAT IT'LL AFFECT YOU ANYMORE!
SOME CAN'T WORK OUT WHAT'S HAPPENED. SOME THINK IT A BAD DREAM. WE HAD A JUDOON HERE ONCE...
...IT PULLED ITS OWN HEAD OFF. YOU'RE WITH THE DOCTOR, RIGHT?
YES, HOW DID YOU KNOW? WHO ARE YOU?
BECAUSE I AM—OR RATHER WAS—THE HORSE LORD OF KHAN.

THINK OF IT, DOCTOR! LIFE-CRIPPLING INJURIES WILL BE A THING OF THE PAST!
JUST UPLOAD YOURSELF INTO A NEW BODY AND TO HELL WITH THE OLD ONE!
OH, I CAN SEE THE ADVANTAGES, DR. RUBIN, BUT I CAN ALSO SEE THE... TEMPTATIONS IT MIGHT GIVE.
WELL, I'D BE LYING IF I DIDN'T ADMIT THAT SOME OF OUR MORE... RICHER... PATRONS ARE INTERESTED IN EXTENDING THEIR LIVES THIS WAY.
TAKE A LOOK AT JARVIS, DOCTOR! SERVED ME FOR DECADES BEFORE ILLNESS TOOK HIS BODY!
NOW HE HAS A NEW BREATH OF LIFE! THE FIRST-EVER TEST SUBJECT!
IT'S A STRANGE SENSATION, I'LL ADMIT, BUT AT THE SAME TIME, I'VE NEVER FELT BETTER.
SOL, YOU COULD BE THE GREATEST THING TO HAPPEN TO HUMANITY.
OR THE WORST THING TO BLIGHT IT.
OH, IT'S NOT JUST HUMANITY, DOCTOR! ALL CREATURES CAN DO THIS! IMAGINE THE PROSPECTS!
A FISH CAN WALK ON LAND! METHANE BREATHERS CAN STAND IN THE SUN!
LOOK, I'LL TELL YOU WHAT— COME AND LOOK AT THE DEVICE. WHATEVER YOU DECIDE, I'LL ABIDE BY.
BUT SEE IT IN WORK, JUST ONCE BEFORE YOU DECIDE.

...AND IF YOU LOOK HERE, YOU'LL SEE THAT ALTHOUGH THE BODY IS IN PERFECT WORKING ORDER, THE BRAINWAVES ARE TOTALLY DEAD.
SO WHEN THESE THINGS GROW, DO THEY GROW A FULL CIRCULATORY SYSTEM? HEART, LUNGS, ALL THAT?
OR IS IT MORE A 'MAGICAL WALKING TURNIP' TYPE OF THING?
HERE—OPEN HIM UP IF YOU WANT. HAVE A LOOK AROUND.
UM, NO THANKS—
—WAIT! DID YOU SEE THAT? I COULD HAVE SWORN THAT HE FLINCHED!
I DON'T THINK SO—IT WOULD HAVE SHOWN UP ON THE SCREEN HERE! THERE ARE NO BRAINWAVE MARKINGS WHATSOEVER!
YEAH, WELL, I WORK FOR THE NATIONAL HEALTH SERVICE, AND SOMETIMES THE MACHINES SIMPLY DON'T GIVE THE FULL STORY.
THE PUPILS ARE CONTRACTING. IT'S INCREDIBLY TINY AMOUNTS, BUT THERE'S DEFINITELY SOMETHING THERE!
THAT CAN'T BE! WE WOULD HAVE PICKED UP SOMETHING!
THIS HOSPITAL SPENDS TOO MUCH TIME LOOKING AT MACHINES AND NOT ENOUGH TIME LOOKING AT THE PATIENTS.
YOU HAVEN'T NOTICED, OR DON'T WANT TO NOTICE...
...THAT THESE PATIENTS ARE STILL HERE IN BODY AND MIND.

IT WAS IN THE MIDDLE OF A SNOWSTORM.
I WAS INJURED. THERE HAD BEEN A BATTLE WITH SOME SPICE RAIDERS WHEN THE SHIPS ARRIVED.
THEY TOOK ME ON BOARD, SAID I WAS ON A MEDICAL VESSEL, BUT I WASN'T. I WAS ON A SHIP THAT HEADED STRAIGHT BACK HERE.
I ONLY SAW SOL RUBIN ONCE, HE CHECKED MY RESTRAINTS AND SAID I WAS A 'GOOD SPECIMEN'.
SPECIMEN OF WHAT?
LOOK AROUND, AMY. THERE'S ONE OF EVERY SENTIENT CREATURE FOR FIVE PARSECS HERE, OUR MINDS TRANSFERRED AND TRAPPED IN VEGETABLE BODIES.
WE'RE SOL RUBIN'S PRIVATE COLLECTION— HIS TOYBOX OF HORRORS.
THEN WE NEED TO GET YOU BACK TO YOUR REAL BODY! THE DOCTOR WILL KNOW WHAT TO DO!
THAT'S THE PROBLEM, I DON'T HAVE A REAL BODY ANYMORE. THE MOMENT RUBIN TRANSFERRED ME, HE MADE ME WATCH IT BURN TO ASH.
I WROTE TO THE DOCTOR, BUT I NEVER SENT THE MESSAGE BECAUSE I KNEW THE RISK IT WOULD BE.
WAIT, WE RECEIVED YOUR MESSAGE!
I KNOW. RUBIN MUST HAVE FOUND IT AND SENT IT ANYWAY.
BUT WHY WOULD HE DO THAT? WHAT POSSIBLE REASON COULD RUBIN HAVE FOR TRICKING US HERE?

OH NO... I HAVE TO TELL HIM. I HAVE TO WARN HIM!
WE LEFT HIM ALONE WITH RUBIN!
THE DOCTOR IS THE LAST OF THE TIME LORDS. THE LAST, AMY.
HE'S A COLLECTOR'S DREAM.
WHAT ARE YOU DOING HERE? TRESPASSER!
DO YOU KNOW WHAT WE DO WITH TRESPASSERS HERE?
RUN AMY! GET TO THE— ARRGHHH!
FZZZZT
GET TO THE DOCTOR!

SO LET ME SEE—THE PATIENT PUTS HIS HAND HERE, AND THE BIOGROWER THERE?
HAND, ARM, FACE—ANY PIECE OF SKIN WORKS FOR THE TRANSFER, OR AS I LIKE TO CALL IT, UPLOAD.
IT'S GOOD WORKMANSHIP. WHERE DO YOU PUT THE BODIES?
BODIES?
YOU KNOW, THE FLESHY REMAINS OF THE PATIENTS WHEN THEY SWAP. DO YOU FREEZE THEM? FIFTEEN-DAY BODY-BACK GUARANTEE? OR ARE THEY DUMPED IN THE TRASH?
I'D ASSUME THE LATTER. AFTER ALL, YOU DON'T WANT PEOPLE TO SEE THE TYPES OF ALIENS YOU'VE BEEN PLAYING WITH, DO YOU?
OH MY. YOU'VE GUESSED MY LITTLE SECRET. HOW DID YOU WORK IT OUT?
WELL, I'VE ALWAYS KNOWN, I JUST NEEDED PROOF.
TRACES OF SLITHEEN, SYCORAX, EVEN GIZHOU DNA SHOWING ON THE TRANSFER GLOBE. YOU REALLY SHOULD CLEAN UP AFTER YOURSELVES.
YOU TOOK A FRIEND OF MINE FOR YOUR TWISTED TROPHY CASE, AND THAT MAKES IT PERSONAL.
YOU CAN'T OUTTHINK ME, OUTSMART ME OR OUTBLUFF ME, SO I SUGGEST—
OH, BUT I ALREADY HAVE, DOCTOR...

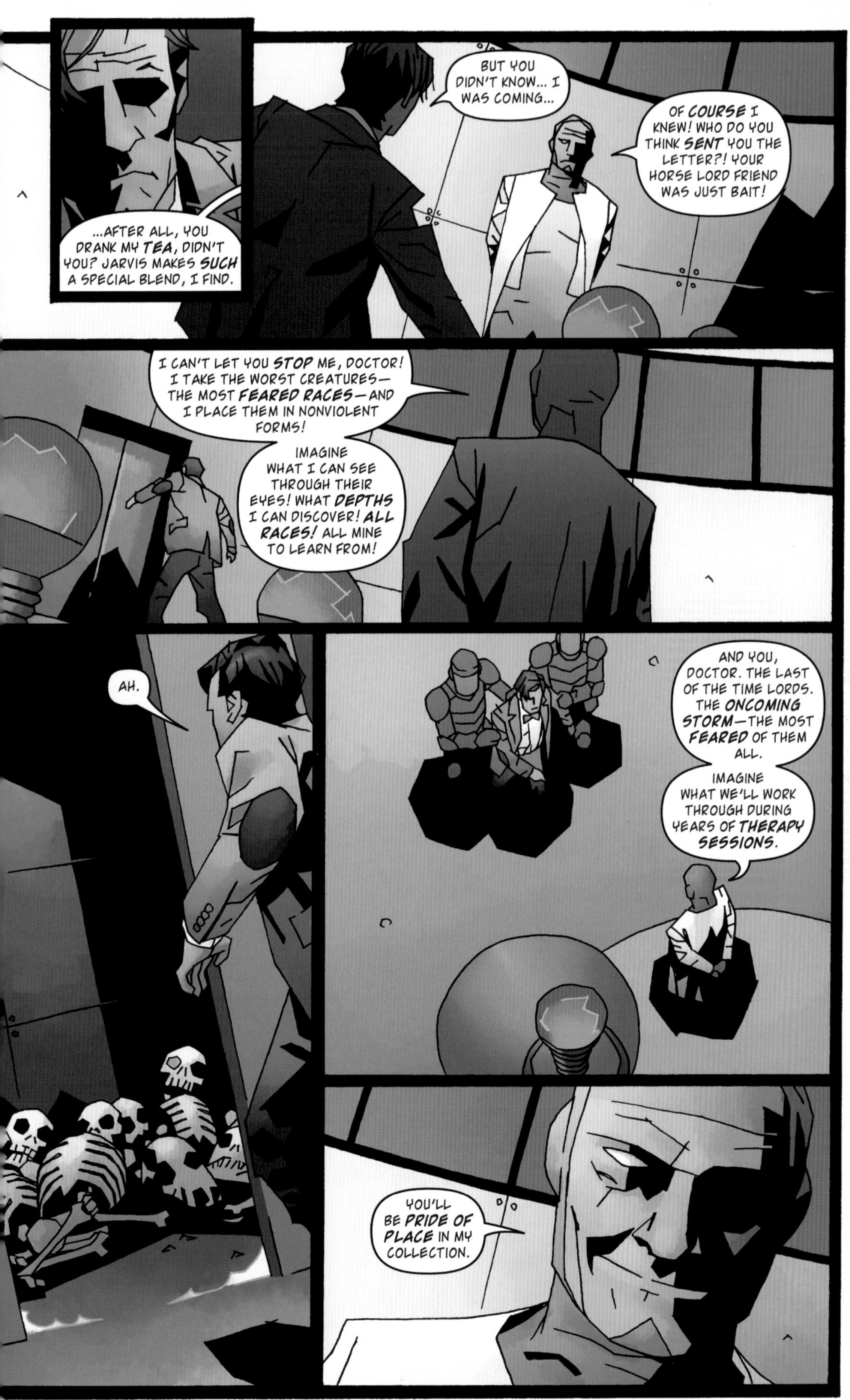
...AFTER ALL, YOU DRANK MY TEA, DIDN'T YOU? JARVIS MAKES SUCH A SPECIAL BLEND, I FIND.
BUT YOU DIDN'T KNOW... I WAS COMING...
OF COURSE I KNEW! WHO DO YOU THINK SENT YOU THE LETTER?! YOUR HORSE LORD FRIEND WAS JUST BAIT!
I CAN'T LET YOU STOP ME, DOCTOR! I TAKE THE WORST CREATURES— THE MOST FEARED RACES—AND I PLACE THEM IN NONVIOLENT FORMS!
IMAGINE WHAT I CAN SEE THROUGH THEIR EYES! WHAT DEPTHS I CAN DISCOVER! ALL RACES! ALL MINE TO LEARN FROM!
AH.
AND YOU, DOCTOR. THE LAST OF THE TIME LORDS. THE ONCOMING STORM—THE MOST FEARED OF THEM ALL.
IMAGINE WHAT WE'LL WORK THROUGH DURING YEARS OF THERAPY SESSIONS.
YOU'LL BE PRIDE OF PLACE IN MY COLLECTION.

RORY! I'VE FOUND SOMETHING TERRIBLE!
ME, TOO! THE BIOGROWERS AREN'T ERASED!
THEY'RE IN SOME KIND OF DEEP HIBERNATION THAT THE MACHINES CAN'T PICK UP!
WE HAVE TO STOP RUBIN FROM STARTING HIS TRANSFERS!
HE'S ALREADY STARTED! THERE'S A ROOM DOWN THERE—TREVOR'S IN IT!
A ROOM FULL OF ALIENS THAT RUBIN'S TRANSFERRED INTO BODIES! HIS OWN SICK COLLECTION!
THAT CAN'T BE! WE'D KNOW!
ARE YOU SURE? THE ROOM I FOUND WAS QUITE WELL GUARDED! I ONLY JUST GOT OUT!
HE TAKES ONE OF EACH RACE, TRANSFERS THEM, AND THEN BURNS THE BODY!
WE NEED TO WARN THE DOCTOR!
LOOK, HELLA, THIS ISN'T YOUR FAULT, BUT YOU'RE A PART OF IT. IF ALIEN MINDS ARE BEING PUT IN BIOGROWERS AND THE BIOGROWERS AWAKEN, WHAT COULD HAPPEN?
TWO MINDS CLAIMING DOMINANCE—IT'D BE A RIOT! AND IF DR. RUBIN IS DOING THIS, THEN HE NEEDS TO BE TOLD OF THESE DISCOVERIES!
BUT IT WOULD TAKE SOMETHING LIKE A MASSIVE ELECTRIC SHOCK TO WAKE ONE!
LIKE A SHOCK STICK? THE GUARDS USED ONE ON TREVOR! WE NEED TO WARN EVERYONE!
LET'S GO THEN! COME ALONG, POND!

AND YOU CAN ROT THERE!
NOBODY SPEAKS TO THE HORSE LORD OF KHAN LIKE THAT. YOU'LL REGRET THAT WHEN I ESCAPE—
SLAM
NNNGGG!
THAT SHOCK... GAVE A KILLER HEADACHE... MUST... GET OUT.
MUST... KILL.

SO, THIS IS YOUR PLAN? TO TURN ME INTO... INTO BROCCOLI? ANOTHER SPECIMEN TO PUT THROUGH YOUR MAZES?
WHAT WILL YOU DO WITH THE BODY? BURN IT LIKE THE OTHERS?
OH NO, DOCTOR! I INTEND TO USE IT! IT'S ONE THING HAVING THE LAST OF THE TIME LORDS AS A TEST SUBJECT...
...BUT TO ACTUALLY BE ONE? I'LL BE A GOD! TELL ME, HOW MANY REGENERATIONS DO YOU HAVE? SEVEN? EIGHT? THINK OF THE YEARS I'LL HAVE!
YOU MIGHT NOT GET WHAT YOU WERE HOPING FOR, RUBIN! I'VE BEEN CARELESS OF LATE—JUST THROWING THEM AWAY!
SO, WHAT? YOU JUST PLUG IN, PLUG OUT, PLUG IN? EVICT ME, AND TAKE POSSESSION?
OH NO, DOCTOR. YOU'RE UNIQUE. THE MACHINE IS BUILT ONLY TO HARNESS ONE INTELLIGENCE—THE BIOGROWERS BEING EMPTY SHELLS AND ALL THAT.
IT'S SUICIDAL TO SWAP INTELLIGENCES—THE MACHINE WOULDN'T B ABLE TO TAKE IT. IT'L SEND AN ELECTRICA FEEDBACK THROUG THE ENTIRE HOSPITA SYSTEM!
THE HUMAN BRAIN CAN'T HANDLE A TIME LORD'S BODY—BELIEVE ME, I'VE SEEN IT HAPPEN. STOP THIS NOW!
I'LL HAVE LIFETIMES TO EXAMINE THE OTHER SAMPLES—THE MOST FEARSOME RACES IN THE UNIVERSE—ALL IN A SIMPLE PLASMATOID FORM!
DOCTOR!
RORY! QUICK! WE NEED TO STOP THIS—

GET OFF HIM! YOU AREN'T GETTING HIM TODAY!
NO! THE PROCESS HAS BEGUN—
ARRRGHHHH!
THUMP
CLICK
FREEDOM. REVENGE.

AMY! DOCTOR!
DR. RUBIN! WHAT DID YOU DO?
HELP US! THE PATIENTS ARE RIOTING! THEY WERE HIT BY A FEEDBACK SURGE AND WENT MAD!
COME ON! GET UP!
TARDIS... GET US... TO TARDIS...
I... I DON'T KNOW WHAT CAME OVER ME! ALL I WANTED TO DO WAS EXAMINE EVIL—TO MAKE THE UNIVERSE BETTER!
THE BIOGROWERS—THEY'RE ALIVE! THEY'RE RIOTING! THE POWER GRID OVERLOADED. THE SECURITY LOCKS HAVE ALL OPENED!
THE BIOGROWERS ARE RIOTING? OR THE PEOPLE YOU STUCK IN THEIR BODIES ARE?
I KNOW EVERYTHING, DOCTOR! AND MORE BESIDES. THE BIOGROWERS' MINDS ARE STILL THERE! THEY'RE NOT EMPTY SHELLS!
AND I PUT THE MOST DANGEROUS CREATURES IN THE WORLD IN THEM!
THEY'LL BE SCHIZOPHRENIC! INSANE! WE'RE DOOMED!
I DID THIS FOR THE RIGHT REASONS! YOU CAN'T JUDGE ME!
DOCTOR! I DID THIS FOR EVERYONE! I ORDER YOU TO HELP US!

AMY! ARE YOU ALL RIGHT?
AMY, TALK TO ME! SAY SOMETHING! I LOVE YOU!
AND I... I LOVE YOU, TOO.
WHAT?
WE NEED TO WORK OUT WHAT'S HAPPENED... WHY DO I FEEL SO... WRONG?
OH NO.
DOCTOR! WHAT'S GOING ON?! WHY DO I LOOK LIKE THIS?
DOCTOR, WHY ARE YOU PRETENDING TO BE AMY?
BECAUSE SHE IS AMY, RORY. OUR MINDS, OUR PERSONALITIES WERE TRANSFERRED WHEN SHE TOUCHED THE PLASMA GLOBE.
THE PLASMA GLOBE THAT THEN BLEW UP.
BUT IF IT'S DESTROYED...

IF IT'S DESTROYED, WE MIGHT HAVE NO OTHER WAY TO CHANGE BACK BEFORE WE STABILISE INTO THESE NEW BODIES...
...WHICH MEANS THAT WE COULD BE STUCK FOREVER!
END: "BODY SNATCHED," PT. 1

AMY, LOOK— WE CAN SORT THIS OUT. I MEAN, WE'VE HAD WEIRDER, RIGHT?
OKAY, MAYBE NOT THIS WEIRD, BUT I'M SURE WE CAN WORK AROUND THIS! RIGHT, DOCTOR?
I HOPE SO TOO, RORY, BUT WITH THE PLASMA GLOBES DESTROYED WE MIGHT BE STUCK IN THESE BODIES INDEFINITELY!
I HOPE NOT. THAT'D MAKE CERTAIN... THINGS... REALLY DIFFICULT!
AND NOT JUST ON THE MARRIAGE FRONT, HOW WOULD I EXPLAIN IT TO MY MUM?
I SUPPOSE IT IS MORE DIFFICULT FOR YOU—TIME LORDS DON'T REALLY WORRY THAT MUCH ABOUT WHAT SEX THEY ARE. ROMANA WAS A TIME LADY AND SHE WAS EASILY EQUAL TO ME.
SOMETIMES, ANYWAY. WHEN SHE DIDN'T USE THE DOG.
I'M A WOMAN NOW. WOMEN ARE COOL.
YEAH, BUT YOU'RE NOT A FEMALE TIME LORD, ARE YOU? YOU'RE A TIME LORD STUCK IN A FEMALE BODY...
...NOW THAT'S JUST WRONG.

LOOK ON THE BRIGHT SIDE, RORY, I'VE ALWAYS WANTED TO BE GINGER!
I DON'T LIKE THIS, DOCTOR. MY HEAD FEELS STRANGE... LIKE IT'S BURSTING OUT OF MY HEAD.

ARE YOU OKAY? YOU NEED ME TO CHECK YOU OVER?
NO, I'M FINE. JUST A LITTLE BIT SHAKEN UP.
SHE'S **NOT**, YOU KNOW. HUMAN BRAIN IN A TIME LORD BODY. IT'S NOT MEANT TO BE.
AND IT'S ALWAYS WORKED OUT **BADLY** IN THE PAST.
SO, LET'S JUST SAY WE NEED TO SORT THIS OUT AS QUICKLY AS POSSIBLE.
RORY, I'M SCARED. I CAN HEAR THE WHOLE UNIVERSE. I THINK I'M GOING MAD.
NO, YOU'RE JUST HEARING WHAT **HE** HEARS ALL THE TIME. MAYBE IT'LL HELP YOU **UNDERSTAND** HIM MORE.
NOT THAT HE **NEEDS** UNDERSTANDING, THAT IS.
BUT KNOW THIS—NO MATTER **WHAT**—I'M HERE FOR YOU.
OHO! STOP HUGGING AND HAVE A LOOK AT THIS!
IT SEEMS OUR DR. RUBIN HAS HAD A SLIGHT CHANGE OF HEART.

FREEDOM. REVENGE.
STILL BRAIN-DEAD, EH? THEN— WHY ARE YOU TRYING TO REGAIN MY BODY—
NNG—NO! MY HEAD! THIS IS MY MIND! I CONTROL THIS BODY!
I AM THE KHAN OF THE HORSE LORDS!
—GAH! GET OFF ME!
CRASH
I NEED TO FIND THE DOCTOR.

DOCTOR! I ADMIT IT. I AY HAVE BEEN RONG HERE. BUT—
—UM...
...YOU ARE THE DOCTOR, RIGHT?
YOU STRAPPED ME TO A TABLE AND TRIED TO STEAL MY BODY. THAT ENOUGH 'ME' FOR YOU?
AND ON THE SUBJECT OF STRAPPING ME DOWN, WHY EXACTLY SHOULD I BE HELPING YOU?
BECAUSE THERE'S ANOTHER DEVICE ON BEDLAM THAT CAN TRANSFER BODIES.
IF YOU HELP ME BRING THE RIOT UNDER CONTROL, I'LL ENSURE YOU SWAP BACK.
HOW DO YOU KNOW THAT WE WANT TO CHANGE BODIES? I PERSONALLY FIND IT QUITE LIBERATING.
YOU CAN REVERSE THIS? HOW? WHAT DO WE NEED TO DO?
RORY, I WAS JUST GOING TO SAY—
I KNOW WHAT YOU WERE JUST GOING TO SAY, DOCTOR. YOU WERE GOING TO KEEP TALKING FOR HALF AN HOUR, TRYING TO CATCH HIM OUT...
...BUT WE DON'T HAVE THAT TIME. AMY IS LOSING, DOCTOR. SHE'S LOSING A BATTLE AGAINST YOUR BODY.
AND SO ARE YOU. YOU'RE NOT FOCUSING PROPERLY, YOU'RE EASILY DISTRACTED...
...WELL, MORE THAN USUAL, THAT IS.
I'VE SPENT TWO MILLENNIA GUARDING HER, DOCTOR. I'VE LOST HER, FOUND HER, AND I LOVE HER.
AND IF THERE'S A WAY TO SAVE HER THAT YOU DON'T TAKE, NO MATTER THE COST...
...I WILL SPEND THE NEXT TWO MILLENNIA HUNTING YOU DOWN.

DOCTOR! WHERE ARE YOU?
YOU! SENTIENT! COME HERE!
COME HERE RIGHT NOW!
I AM THOTH OF THE RE'NAR. LIKE YOU, I WAS PLACED IN THIS PRISON OF A BODY WHILE MY BODY WAS DESTROYED.
I FIGHT TO STOP THIS HAPPENING TO MY BROTHERS. WILL YOU JOIN US?
WHAT, ALL CHUMS UNTIL THE POINT THAT OUR INTERSPECIES HATRED RISES AND OVERWHELMS OUR NEED TO HELP EACH OTHER? NO, THANK YOU.
RE'NAR AND JU'WES, ENOCHIAN AND SATURNYNIANS—WHO KNOWS WHAT ELSE WE HAVE HERE. CHELONIANS? AN ICE WARRIOR OR TWO?
AND I'M SUPPOSED TO BELIEVE THAT YOU'VE ALL MADE NICE AND BECOME FIRM FRIENDS?
WHY NOT? THIS IS A SITUATION NONE OF US HAVE BEEN IN. ALL DISPARATE PEOPLE...
...YET NOW ONE RACE. ASK THE FIRST. JARVIS.
HAVE YOU FELT THE OTHER MIND IN YOUR BODY? THE PLASMATOID ONE?

IT WAKES. THE ELECTRICAL FEEDBACK HAS STIMULATED IT. AND IT WANTS ITS **BODY** BACK.
I SPENT YEARS WORKING WITH RUBIN. I KNOW HIS SECRETS. I KNOW OF A **SECOND** DEVICE.
I HAVE NO WISH TO DIE, BUT IF WE CAN TRANSFER BODIES WITH THE HUMAN STAFF, WE CAN LEAVE **THEM** TO DEAL WITH THE EVICTION!
AND HOW DO WE DO THAT? ASK POLITELY?
NO, WE MAKE CHANGES TO THE REACTOR AND **FORCE THEM** TO AGREE. JARVIS KNOWS THE CODES.
LIFE IN A NEW BODY OVER **DEATH BY FIRE.**
I DON'T KNOW. THE DOCTOR—
—IS IN ANOTHER BODY WHILE A GIRL IS IN HIS. THE PROCEDURE WORKS...
...WE ARE ALL **LIVING EXAMPLES** OF THAT.
WE FIGHT FOR OUR IDENTITIES! WE FIGHT TO STAY ALIVE!
WHO'S **WITH ME**? LET'S STORM THE REACTOR!
WHY NOT? ANYTHING'S BETTER THAN THIS!
FREEDOM. REVENGE.

THIS CROSS SECTION OF PLASMATOID GROWTH IS FASCINATING! A COPLANAR DOUBLE HYDROCARBON BOND...
...THIS IS ETHYLENE! DR. RUBIN, YOU HAD THE BIOGROWERS SENDING CHEMICAL MESSAGES TO EACH OTHER, PROVING SENTIENCE—AND YOU STILL DID THIS TO THEM?
DID WHAT? SO THEY MADE SOME GAS? WHO CARES?! THEY'RE BRAIN-DEAD!
THE BIOGROWERS WEREN'T COMMUNICATING, DOCTOR, HE WAS FORCING THEM TO CREATE THE CHEMICAL.
MIX ETHYLENE WITH OXYGEN, IT'S A POWERFUL ANAESTHETIC. YOU'D LOOK ALMOST LIFELESS.
YOU'D LOOK LIKE THEY DO.
SO I KEPT THEM SEDATED! WHY HAVE ZOMBIES WALKING AROUND WHEN YOU CAN HAVE THEM SITTING?
THE ELECTRICAL CHARGE STIMULATED THEM, OVERCAME THE DOSAGE!
ALL THIS TIME, I THOUGHT YOU WERE ONE OF THE GREATEST MINDS IN THE WORLD!
WHAM
—THEY WERE NOTHING BUT LIES!
TELL ME HOW YOU CREATED THE ETHYLENE IN THE PLASMATOIDS, RUBIN. SHOW US HOW TO RECREATE IT.
BECAUSE THE ONLY WAY TO STOP THEM—IS TO DO AGAIN WHAT YOU'VE ALWAYS BEEN DOING TO THEM.

ATTENTION STAFF AND VISITORS OF BEDLAM. I'M SORRY TO TELL YOU THIS, BUT THERE'S GOING TO HAVE TO BE A LITTLE CHANGEOVER PROCESS.
IF YOU COULD ALL MAKE YOUR WAY TO THE COMMON AREA, WE'LL ENSURE THAT YOUR MINDS WILL BE HOUSED IN THE BRIGHTEST OF BIOFORMS.
BEHOLD! HE REACTOR!
I THINK YOU'LL FIND THAT OUR BARGAINING CHIP JUST GOT BIGGER.
THE ALTERNATIVE TO THIS IS, OF COURSE, A FIERY DEATH AFTER WE IMPLODE THE REACTOR.
I THINK WE CAN BOTH AGREE THAT OUR OPTION IS THE MORE HUMANE OF THE TWO.
OH, AND WE'D LIKE DR. RUBIN TO BE THE FIRST PERSON TO ATTEND US. IT'S ONLY FAIR FOR HIM TO SEE THE FRUITS OF HIS LABOURS.
DAMN YOU, JARVIS! I SAVED YOU! YOU SHOULD LOVE ME FOR IT!
USING A STRONG SUBSONIC PULSE THROUGH THE SYSTEM GRID, WE SHOULD BE ABLE TO TRIGGER AN IMMEDIATE ETHYLENE REACTION...
...RENDERING THE PLASMATOIDS INERT. WE JUST NEED A STRONG SONIC SOURCE—
THAT WE HAVE IN EXCESS, NURSE HELLA.

AMY!
AH, DOCTOR, AT LAST! I THOUGHT I'D NEVER FIND YOU!
SORRY, TREVOR, BUT IT'S ME. AMY.
THE DOCTOR'S NOW THE GIRL IN THE BOW TIE.
OF COURSE. FORGIVE ME FOR SURPRISING YOU.
THE LUNATICS HAVE TAKEN OVER THE ASYLUM, DOCTOR. I DO HOPE YOU HAVE A PLAN.
DR. RUBIN HAS A BACKUP NETWORK OUTSIDE THE ASYLUM. IF WE CAN DIVERT THE POWER, WE CAN SEND A NARROW BEAM SONIC PULSE INTO THE SYSTEM.
IT'LL FEEDBACK IN THE SAME WAY THAT THE ELECTRICITY DID, BUT IT'LL ONLY AFFECT ONE PART OF THE BIOGROWER.
I'M SORRY, BUT IT'LL AFFECT YOU, TOO.
FINE. DO WHAT NEEDS TO BE DONE. I WILL ASSIST.
VEGETATION COULD NEVER LEAD THE HORSE LORDS, ANYWAY. I'D BE NOTHING MORE THAN...
...SIDE SALAD.

FREEDOM. REVENGE.
WHY DO THEY NOT REPLY? DO THEY THINK WE TOY WITH THEM? I AM NOT USED TO BEING IGNORED!
SEND THEM A MESSAGE!
WHAT MESSAGE? BLOW UP THE REACTOR A LITTLE?
WE HAVE LOST, THOTH! THEY CALLED OUR BLUFF AND WE FOLDED! I COULD NEVER GO THROUGH WITH HARMING THESE PEOPLE—THEY WERE MY FRIENDS—
YOUR FRIENDS DID THIS TO YOU! WE ARE YOUR FAMILY!
CHLOROPHYLL IS THICKER THAN WATER!
WE ARE UNDER ATTACK!
FREEDOM. REVENGE.
GRAARGGHH!

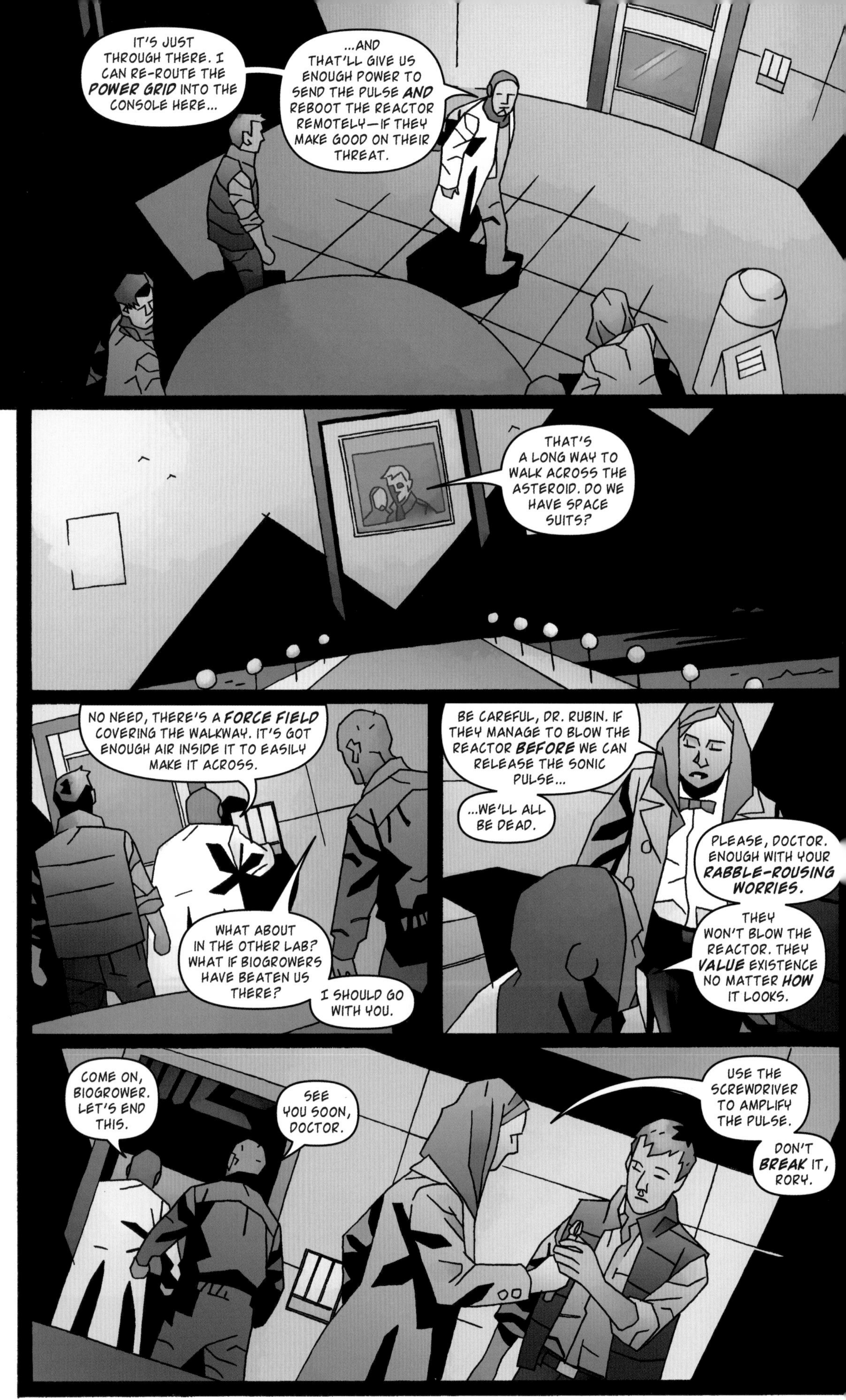

IT'S JUST THROUGH THERE. I CAN RE-ROUTE THE POWER GRID INTO THE CONSOLE HERE...
...AND THAT'LL GIVE US ENOUGH POWER TO SEND THE PULSE AND REBOOT THE REACTOR REMOTELY—IF THEY MAKE GOOD ON THEIR THREAT.
THAT'S A LONG WAY TO WALK ACROSS THE ASTEROID. DO WE HAVE SPACE SUITS?
NO NEED, THERE'S A FORCE FIELD COVERING THE WALKWAY. IT'S GOT ENOUGH AIR INSIDE IT TO EASILY MAKE IT ACROSS.
WHAT ABOUT IN THE OTHER LAB? WHAT IF BIOGROWERS HAVE BEATEN US THERE?
I SHOULD GO WITH YOU.
BE CAREFUL, DR. RUBIN. IF THEY MANAGE TO BLOW THE REACTOR BEFORE WE CAN RELEASE THE SONIC PULSE...
...WE'LL ALL BE DEAD.
PLEASE, DOCTOR. ENOUGH WITH YOUR RABBLE-ROUSING WORRIES.
THEY WON'T BLOW THE REACTOR. THEY VALUE EXISTENCE NO MATTER HOW IT LOOKS.
COME ON, BIOGROWER. LET'S END THIS.
SEE YOU SOON, DOCTOR.
USE THE SCREWDRIVER TO AMPLIFY THE PULSE.
DON'T BREAK IT, RORY.

DOCTOR! THERE'S SOMETHING WRONG! DR. RUBIN IS SUFFOCATING!
THE FORCE FIELD IS DOWN! THERE'S NO OXYGEN!
WE CAN'T GET TO HIM!

HELLO, DOCTOR. SORRY YOU HAD TO SEE THAT. YOU SEE, I HAD TO GET OVER HERE WITHOUT DR. RUBIN.
DOCTOR!
AND LET'S FACE IT, HE DESERVED EVERYTHING HE GOT.
IT WAS I WHO CALLED FOR YOU TO COME AND HELP, DOCTOR.
I KNEW RUBIN WOULD FIND IT, THOUGH, AND I ALSO KNEW YOU WERE TOO GOOD A TEMPTATION FOR HIM TO PASS UP.
BUT IT WASN'T RUBIN WHO WANTED YOUR BODY—I WANTED IT.
THINK OF THE POSSIBILITIES! A TIME LORD AND HORSE LORD! I'D BE IMMORTAL! AND YOU WASTED IT ON A GIRL!
SO HERE'S MY OFFER TO YOU.
ONCE I RAISE THE FORCE SHIELD AGAIN, SEND THE GIRL IN THE TIME LORD BODY OVER.
WE'LL SWAP BODIES AND THEN I'LL STOP THE RIOTS. I'LL ARRANGE THE SONIC PULSE.
BUT WHY, TREVOR? WE WERE FRIENDS!
BECAUSE, AS YOU SAID EARLIER, IF YOU CREATE A SONIC PULSE, IT'LL PUT ME IN HIBERNATION AS WELL. SOL WAS RIGHT. I VALUE MY EXISTENCE TOO MUCH.
SO YOU HAVE FIVE MINUTES TO MAKE YOUR MIND UP WHILE I SET UP THE PLASMA GLOBES. YOUR BODY... OR EVERYONE'S LIVES?

THE REACTOR.
KEEP THEM AWAY! DON'T LET THEM STOP US!
THE HUMANS WON'T GIVE US WHAT WE WANT! THE REACTOR MUST BE DESTROYED!
ONLY IN DEATH CAN WE WIN THIS BATTLE! THIS IS THE RE'NAR WAY!
IT IS NOT MY WAY, THOTH! WE HAVE TO GIVE THEM MORE TIME—
I AM SICK OF GIVING THEM TIME.
SNAP
ACARI! ENOCIANS! SATURNYNIANS! TODAY WE GO DOWN IN HISTORY!
TODAY WE DIE AS FREE SPECIES.
ACTIVATE
AUTO DESTRUCT
CLICK
YES

WHAT DO WE DO, DOCTOR?! I DON'T WANT TO BE BROCCOLI!
TREVOR'S GOING TO BE BUSY FOR A COUPLE OF MINUTES, AND HE THINKS THAT HE'S SAFE THERE WITH THE OXYGEN GONE.
BUT HE HASN'T COUNTED ON ONE THING.
CURRENTLY, YOU'RE A TIME LORD, AMY. WHICH MEANS THAT IF YOU PUT YOUR MIND TO IT, YOU CAN DO TIME LORD THINGS.
TELEPATHY BY CONTACT. YOU CAN SENSE THE UNIVERSE. A WHOLE LOAD OF THINGS THAT CURRENTLY CROWD YOUR MIND, HURT YOU.
BUT YOU ALSO HAVE A RESPIRATORY BYPASS SYSTEM. YOU CAN HOLD YOUR BREATH IN THE DEPTHS OF SPACE.
I CAN'T TELL YOU TO DO THIS, BUT IT'S THE ONLY HOPE WE HAVE. TREVOR IS DISTRACTED WHILE HE THINKS THAT HE'S SAFE.
GET IN THERE NOW AND TURN THE OXYGEN ON BEFORE HE CAN STOP YOU. THEN WE CAN GET ACROSS AND HELP YOU.
YOU CAN DO THIS, AMY, AND WE'LL BE RIGHT BEHIND YOU.
I'LL ALWAYS BE WITH YOU, NO MATTER WHAT YOU LOOK LIKE.
IT'S JUST HOLDING MY BREATH. HOW HARD CAN THAT BE?
THAT'S THE AMELIA POND I KNOW! FISH FINGERS AND CUSTARD!

CONTACT!
THUNK
ARGH!
HSSSST
HOW DID YOU MANAGE—
WHAT DID YOU DO TO ME?! THE IMAGES...
...THE DOCTOR WOULD NEVER HAVE...
YEAH... BUT YOU FORGOT ONE THING, TREVOR...
...I'M NOT THE DOCTOR.
WHAM
HORSE LORD OF KHAN, INDEED.

GOOD WORK, POND! NOW TO SWITCH THE POWER ACROSS—
—AH.
'AH'? IT'S NEVER GOOD WHEN YOU SAY 'AH'.
YES, I KNOW. THEY'VE STARTED THE REACTOR CORE IMPLOSION ALREADY.
THE PULSE WILL STOP IT BY REBOOTING THE CORE NETWORK THE EXACT MOMENT IT HITS ZERO...
...BUT BY DOING THAT WE WON'T HAVE ENOUGH ENERGY TO CHANGE BACK. THE REACTOR WILL TAKE ALL THE ENERGY TO REBOOT.
RORY, GO WITH HELLA AND GET READY TO FIRE THE PULSE. WE MIGHT BE ABLE TO FIND ENOUGH ENERGY TO STABILISE THESE BODIES.
WHAT'LL HAPPEN TO US WHEN THE PULSE HITS?
WILL IT AFFECT US?
I DON'T KNOW, POND. ALL I KNOW IS THAT—
—OF COURSE! IDIOT TIME LORD! WELL, HUMAN, SO THAT'S EXPECTED OF ME!
WE CAN FEED THE CANCELLED REACTOR IMPLOSION BUILDUP INTO THE PLASMA GLOBES! AS WE REBOOT, WE SIPHON OFF THE EXTRA ENERGY!
WHAT WILL THAT DO?
HONESTLY? PROBABLY OVERLOAD AND KILL US.
BUT WHO WANTS TO LIVE FOREVER, ANYWAY?!

TEN, NINE, EIGHT—
SEVEN, SIX, FIVE, FOUR—
SONIC PULSE READY TO GO!
REMEMBER TO MAKE SURE IT'S EXACTLY ON ZERO! IT'S THE ONLY WAY TO STOP THE REACTOR!
THREE, TWO, ONE—
READY, POND?
NO!
MARK!
MMMMMMM
SYSTEM REBOOT. SYSTEM REBOOT.
AIIEEEEEE!
ARRGHHHHH!

AMY! ARE YOU ALL RIGHT?
URGHHH...
THANK GOD! I DON'T KNOW WHAT I'D DO WITHOUT YOU!
I DON'T CARE WHAT YOU LOOK LIKE. I LOVE YOU, AMY! WE'LL MAKE THIS WORK... ALTHOUGH YOUR MUM WON'T BE HAPPY!
MMMPH!
AS PASSIONATE AS THAT WAS, RORY, DON'T YOU THINK YOU SHOULD BE KISSING YOUR WIFE, NOT ME?
OH NO. DO IT AGAIN BUT DO IT... SLOWER.
GREAT. ALWAYS THE LAST TO KNOW, I AM.
AW, DON'T BE A GRUMP, I THOUGHT YOUR WORDS WERE SWEET!
AND IF YOU WANT, YOU CAN ALWAYS KISS ME, TOO!

SO, IT'S ALL YOUR PROBLEM NOW, IS IT?
YES, DOCTOR. THE BOARD WERE IMPRESSED WITH MY CONDUCT AND HAVE ASKED ME TO STAY ON AS WE WORK OUT WHAT TO DO.
POLICE PUBLIC CALL BOX
WE'VE TAKEN RUBIN'S EXPERIMENTS AND PUT THEM INTO MAXIMUM SECURITY, IN CASE THEY WAKE AGAIN.
WE'LL USE THE GLOBE TECHNOLOGY TO REMOVE THEM FROM THE BIOGROWERS AND PUT THEM IN ARTIFICIAL HOUSING UNTIL WE WORK OUT WHAT TO DO NEXT WITH THEM.
THERE'S TALK OF CLONING THE REMAINS OF THEIR ORIGINAL BODIES, BUT THAT'S YEARS OFF.
AND THE BIOGROWERS?
WE'LL REAWAKEN THEM SLOWLY, REINTEGRATE THEM INTO SOCIETY. THEY HAVE A LOT OF USE LEFT IN THEM.
THANKS FOR EVERYTHING, RORY.
'THANKS FOR EVERYTHING, RORY'.
I DON'T KNOW... FLIRTING WITH NURSES, KISSING TIME LORDS...
PUBLIC CALL BOX
CAN WE GO NOW, PLEASE? LIKE RIGHT NOW?
A HOLIDAY MIGHT BE AN IDEA. A HOT BEACH, SITTING BY A POOL, READING A BOOK...
IN A BIKINI? YOU'D BE WEARING A BIKINI?
DOCTOR, I REALLY THINK THAT AMY NEEDS THIS AFTER ALL THE TRAUMA.

POLICE PUBLIC CALL BOX

VWORP VWORP

THE END.

POLICE BOX
POLICE BOX
POLICE BOX
POLICE BOX

Silent Knight

THE NAUGHTY LIST
JEFF THOMPSON
SHAUN LYO
RICK
ARSHALL
ARNABY
WARDS
AARON
ARONSON

POLICE PUBLIC CALL BOX
FOR SANTA x

to RORY
AND AMY
POND

to RORY
AND AMY
POND
WILLIAMS

SUPER
LOTTO
31ST DECEMBER
09, 12,
32, 29,
41, 38

IRATE
SS-UP

POLICE TELEPHONE
FREE
FOR USE OF
PUBLIC
ADVICE & ASSISTANCE
OBTAINABLE IMMEDIATLY
OFFICER & CARS
RESPOND TO ALL CALLS
PULL TO OPEN

TO THE DOCTOR - FROM SANTA

POLICE CALL BOX
POLICE TELEPHONE
FREE
FOR USE OF
PUBLIC
INCIDENTLY, A HAPPY CHRISTMAS TO ALL OF YOU AT HOME!
TELEPHONE
REE
USE OF
BLIC

POLICE BOX
FREE
PUBLIC
PULL TO OPEN

POLICE PUBLIC CALL BOX
POLICE PUBLIC CALL BOX

POLICE PUBLIC CALL BOX
POLICE PUBLIC CALL BOX

POLICE PUBLIC CALL BOX
POLICE PUBLIC CALL BOX

POLICE PUBLIC CALL BOX
POLICE PUBLIC CALL BOX
CRASH
FLUUUUUGEL

WELL, THAT'S ONE WAY TO MAKE A FRIEND.
HELLO! I'M THE DOCTOR!
RUN, DOCTOR, RUN
BY JOSHUA HALE FIALKOV AND BLAIR SHEDD
YOU... YOU RUINED MY MASTERPIECE.
DID I? I'M SORRY.
I DON'T THINK I DID.
WHAT MASTERPIECE, PRECISELY?

KILL THE ART-MURDERER!
HE HAS VERY LITTLE CLASS OR APPRECIATION FOR FINE THINGS!
AND HE'S STANDING UPSIDE-DOWN!

NOW HOLD ON A TIC, LET'S WORK THIS—

—RIGHT. TALK LATER.

GRAVITATIONAL SHIFTERS? FANTASTIC!

HM. RIGHT.
UP AND DOWN.
SHOULD BE EASY ENOUGH.

AHA!

GAH!

HURM.
GERONIMO?

GRAVITATIONAL ADJUSTMENTS.
CENTRIFUGAL FORCE IS MEANINGLESS, AND THE NEWTONIAN PRINCIPLES ARE GONE.
SO THAT MEANS—

BEEEEEEEEEEEEEEE

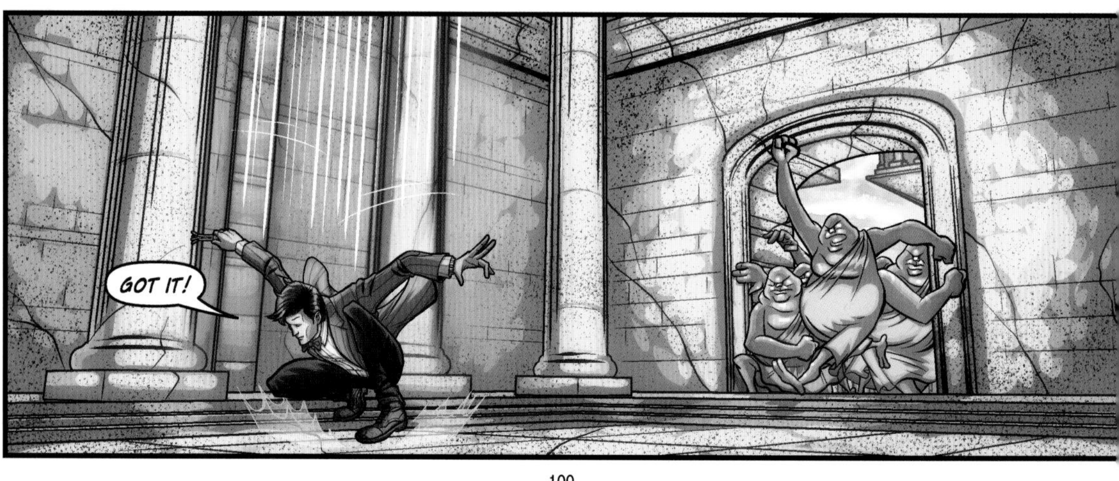
GOT IT!

STOP!

WHAT EXACTLY IS GOING ON HERE?
WHAT IS THIS PLANET?

WHAT'S HE ON ABOUT?
HE KILLED FARIAH JAZBLOOM.

...RIGHT. I JUST NEED TO GET BACK TO MY SHIP. I CAN BE OUT OF YOUR HAIR IN A BLINK.
IF YOU JUST...
SIGH

AH, I SEEM TO HAVE GONE SIDEWAYS A BIT.

HAHA!
THINK VARIABLE DENSITY... THINK VARIABLE DENSITY... THINK VARIABLE DENSITY...
FANTASTIC!

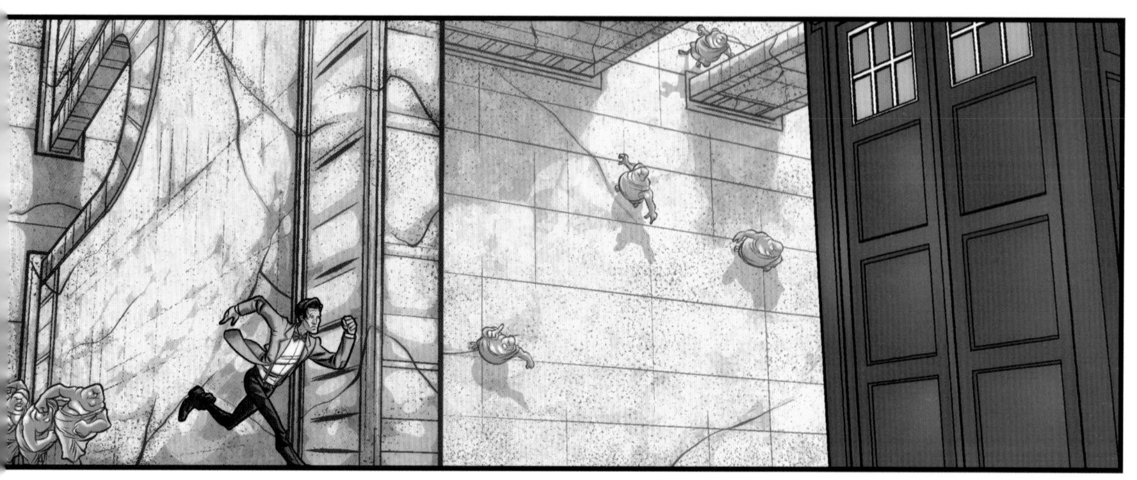

OH... NO...

ARE YOU OKAY?

AREN'T YOU TRYING TO KILL ME?
YES.
SO, WHY DOES IT MATTER HOW I'M DOING?
I MEAN, I'M...
...NEVER MIND. COME ON! COME GET ME!

WHAT'S THE MATTER? WHY AREN'T YOU SCALING DOWN THE—
—AHA!

PROTOMOLECULAR SOFT SPOT!

NOW THAT'S COOL.
TELL ME, UP THERE, THIS... UH... WORLD. IT'S BUILT ON A GASEOUS BALL, YES?
YES.

IT MUST BE TOUGH NOT KNOWING UP FROM DOWN AND LEFT FROM RIGHT, YES?
IT'S NOT AS BAD AS ALL THAT.

REALLY? EXPLAIN?
POLICE BOX

WELL, DOWN IS ALWAYS DOWN FOR US, EVEN WHEN IT'S UP.
AND, FURTHERMORE, LEFT IS ALWAYS LEFT, EVEN WHEN IT'S RIGHT.
OH.
POLICE BOX

LOOK, I CLEARLY DID SOMETHING AWFUL TO... UH... SORRY... YOUR NAME AGAIN?
FARIAH JAZBLOOM.
RIGHT.

SO, HOWSABOUT I FIX IT? I MEAN, THIS IS FUN AND ALL, BUT, REALLY, WOULDN'T YOU RATHER HAVE, WELL, A PROPER UP-AND-DOWN WORLD?
POLICE BOX

YOU FORGIVE ME MY CRIMES AGAINST ART AND, UH, TROMBONING, AND I'LL MAKE YOUR WORLD LIKE EVERY OTHER PLANET IN THE UNIVERSE.

DEAL?

POLICE PUBLIC CALL BOX

POLICE PUBLIC CALL BOX
THAT'S ALL, FOLKS!
POLICE TELEPHONE FREE
THE END.

ANOTHER BEAUTIFUL DAY, HAROLD.
INDEED IT IS, TOM.

DON'T FORGET THE CAKE SALE THIS SUNDAY.
I'M WHIPPING UP A SPECIAL BATCH OF MY PRIZE-WINNING CHOCOLATE COOKIES.
WOULDN'T MISS IT FOR THE WORLD, MRS. RUNSON.

OH, YES.
A BEAUTIFUL DAY, INDEED.

LOVELY LITTLE VILLAGE YOU'VE GOT HERE...

DOWN TO EARTH

BY MATTHEW DOW SMITH AND MITCH GERADS

THAT PERCEPTION FILTER MIGHT WORK ON THE LOCALS, BUT BELIEVE ME...

...I'M NOT A LOCAL.
WWRRRRRR

DON'T...
WWRRRRRR

...OH, DEAR.

NOW.
WHERE WAS I?
AH, YES...
...WHO ARE YOU? AND WHY ARE YOU HERE?

HAROLD.
HAROLD LUMLEY.

A TRYLONIAN, UNLESS I MISS MY GUESS.
NASTY RACE, THE TRYLONIANS.
BAD HABIT OF INVADING OTHER PLANETS.

NEVER MET ONE NAMED HAROLD BEFORE.
BIT UNUSUAL, DON'T YOU THINK?
MY NAME IS HAROLD NOW.
POLICE TELEPH
FREE
FOR USE OF
PUBLIC
ADVICE & ASSISTAN
OBTAINABLE IMMEDIA
OFFICER & CARS
RESPOND TO ALL CA
PULL TO OP

A TRYLONIAN LIGHT YEARS FROM HOME, HIDING BEHIND A PERCEPTION FILTER.
WHICH BRINGS ME BACK TO MY OTHER QUESTION...
...WHY ARE YOU HERE?

YOU WOULDN'T UNDERSTAND.
TRY ME.

IT WAS A LONG TIME AGO...
'...I WAS STILL LUM-TEE BACK THEN, A COMMANDER IN THE TRYLONIAN SPACE FLEET.
'WE HAD JUST LAUNCHED AN OFFENSIVE AGAINST THE ZORIAN HOMEWORLD.
'IT WAS A BLOODY BATTLE.
'BUT THEN, AREN'T THEY ALL?
'WE WORE THEIR DEFENSES DOWN WITH WAVE AFTER WAVE OF OUR BATTLE CRUISERS.
'SACRIFICING ENTIRE SQUADRONS OF STAR FIGHTERS TO CREATE A PATH FOR OUR GROUND FORCES.
'AND THEN, WITH VICTORY WITHIN OUR GRASP...
'...YOU APPEARED'.

YOU CAME FROM NOWHERE, IN THAT BLUE BOX OF YOURS.
ONE MAN AGAINST AN ENTIRE BATTLE FLEET, AND YOU SENT US PACKING LIKE WOUNDED DOGS.

THE MYSTERIOUS DOCTOR.
THE MOST FEARED WARRIOR IN THE UNIVERSE.

MY SHIP WAS TOO DAMAGED TO MAKE IT BACK HOME WITH THE REST OF THE FLEET.
I BARELY REACHED THIS PLANET.
CRASHED NOT FAR FROM HERE. FIFTY YEARS AGO, ALMOST TO THE DAY.

AND YOU'VE BEEN HIDING HERE EVER SINCE?
LONG TIME TO BE ON YOUR OWN.
WHAT HAVE YOU BEEN DOING ALL THIS TIME?

PATIENTLY WAITING TO BE RESCUED?
PLANNING A ONE-MAN INVASION OF THE ENTIRE PLANET?

I CAN SHOW YOU, IF YOU'D LIKE.

TELL ME THAT'S NOT WHAT I THINK IT IS.
A TRYLONIAN STAR FIGHTER, CLASS II.
MY SHIP.

THERE WASN'T MUCH LEFT AFTER I CRASHED, BUT I'VE BEEN REBUILDING HER, PIECE BY PIECE.

THAT INTERESTING ENERGY SIGNATURE I PICKED UP...
...AN ION-CONTAINMENT DRIVE?

WITH A FEW MINOR IMPROVEMENTS.

THEN HERE'S WHAT I DON'T UNDERSTAND...
...THIS IS A FULLY FUNCTIONAL TRYLONIAN STAR FIGHTER...
...WELL, A MOSTLY FUNCTIONAL TRYLONIAN STAR FIGHTER...
...YOU COULD RETURN TO YOUR PLANET ANY TIME YOU LIKE.
OR TAKE CONTROL OF THIS WORLD THREE TIMES OVER WITHOUT EVEN STOPPING TO REFILL THE TANKS.
SO, WHAT IS IT DOING SITTING IN AN OLD BARN, GATHERING DUST?
THIS PLANET IS MY HOME NOW.
WHY WOULD I WANT TO LEAVE IT?
OR DESTROY IT?
THEN WHY REBUILD YOUR SHIP IN THE FIRST PLACE?
WHY NOT LEAVE THE PAST BURIED?
HAVE YOU EVER FLOWN A STAR FIGHTER, DOCTOR?

I MAY HAVE LOST MY STOMACH FOR WAR, BUT I NEVER LOST THE NEED TO FLY.
FOR FORTY YEARS, I'VE BEEN DREAMING OF THE DAY WHEN I COULD SOAR THROUGH THE SKY AGAIN.

BUT NOW THAT IT'S FINALLY HERE, I DON'T DARE.
THE ENTIRE VILLAGE WOULD SEE.
ALL MY WONDERFUL NEW FRIENDS WOULD FIND OUT WHAT I AM.

THEY'D TURN AGAINST ME.
YOUR PERCEPTION FILTER...
...CAN I SEE?

HANDY BIT OF TECHNOLOGY, PERCEPTION FILTERS...
...YOU CAN HIDE IN PLAIN SIGHT.
THE VIEWER ONLY SEES WHAT THEY EXPECT TO SEE.

AND IF YOU MAKE IT POWERFUL ENOUGH...

'...YOU CAN HIDE JUST ABOUT ANYTHING.'

FWWOOOOOSSSSHHHH

WOO-HOO!
'...BUT THEY'LL SEE AN OLD WORLD WAR II FIGHTER OUT FOR A SUNDAY AFTERNOON SPIN.
'OR A CROP DUSTER SPRAYING THE FIELDS'.
WHATEVER THEY EXPECT TO SEE ALL THE WAY UP HERE.
'...I DO HAVE MY MOMENTS'.

SO, WHAT NOW?
WELL, NO MORE JOY-RIDING, FOR ONE THING.
YOU'RE GOING TO NEED THAT PERCEPTION FILTER TO KEEP BLENDING IN HERE.

CAN'T HAVE A BLUE-SKINNED TRYLONIAN WANDERING THROUGH THE VILLAGE.
YOU'D START A RIOT.

I DON'T UNDERSTAND.
YOU AREN'T GOING TO MAKE ME GO BACK HOME?
SAVE THE PLANET FROM ALIEN INVASION I CAN DO...

...BUT MAKING SOMEONE GO HOME SEEMS A BIT OUT OF MY LEAGUE.
BESIDES...

OLICE TELEPHONE
FREE
FOR USE OF
PUBLIC
VICE & ASSISTANCE
INABLE IMMEDIATELY
...LOOKS TO ME LIKE YOU'RE HOME, ALREADY.
THE END.

6
Dear Mum and Dad,
Hiya! So, yeah, it's been ages, hasn't it? Sorry about that. life's a bit hectic when you're lost in time and space. God, that sounds bad, doesn't it? We're not lost, I promise. The Doctor knows what he's doing.
Well...
TUESDAY
Story, art and colors by Dan McDaid
Color assist by Deborah McCumiskey

...most of the time.
DOCTOR. KEEPING WELL, I TRUST?
OH, I'VE BEEN BETTER. THE FOOD'S TERRIBLE, THE ROOM'S DRAUGHTY, AND THE BUNK IS MADE OF LUMPS OF... STUFF.

MY APOLOGIES, DOCTOR...
Wait. Okay, just to clarify, I wasn't here for this bit. The Doctor told me about it afterwards. He was in a prison cell on... Gibraltar? I think? Anyway, this was 1958, and the man holding the Doctor prisoner is an exiled royal called...
...SIR REGINALD TROUPE. AT YOUR SERVICE.

OH, I KNOW WHO YOU ARE. AND BELIEVE IT OR NOT, I KNOW ALL ABOUT YOUR PLAN. AND I'M GOING TO STOP YOU.
FROM IN HERE? I DON'T THINK SO. NO, DOCTOR, I THINK YOU'LL BE IN HERE TILL YOUR BONES HAVE TURNED TO DUST.

AS FOR ME, I WILL SOON BE TAKING MY RIGHTFUL PLACE AS KING OF ENGLAND AND EMPEROR OF THE WORLD. AND I DOUBT I WILL THINK ABOUT YOU EVER AGAIN.

GOODBYE.
KLUK

RIGHT!

SPRINGS, YES, THAT'S IT.

POWER! LOTS AND **LOTS** OF POWER!

TRANSMITTER, TRANSMITTER...
YES, THIS SHOULD DO THE TRICK...
HA HA, IT **WORKS!** BRILLIANT! AND NO ONE WAS AROUND TO SEE IT... NEVER MIND.
HELLO? DOCTOR CALLING **AMELIA POND**, ARE YOU THERE, POND?

SOME KIND OF FILAMENT. THAT'LL BE ESSENTIAL...

ARE YOU THERE, POND?

POND? CAN YOU HEAR ME, POND?
ACTUALLY, DOCTOR...

...THIS ISN'T A GOOD TIME!
WHAT'S HAPPENING?
I'M ON THE VANGUARD SHIP OF THE VROON WAR FLEET, AND I'VE RAISED A RESISTANCE FORCE, WHICH WASN'T EASY BECAUSE THE WORKERS ON THIS SHIP ARE A WEE BIT OLD-FASHIONED ABOUT WOMEN, BY WHICH I MEAN THEY DON'T LISTEN TO US AT ALL, ABOUT ANYTHING, AND...
POND!
WE'VE GOT A PROBLEM. THE VROON GUARDS ARE ARMED TO THE TEETH, AND ALL WE'VE GOT IS MOPS, BUCKETS, AND COOKING UTENSILS. THE MOST DANGEROUS WEAPON WE'VE GOT IS A SPORK.
A SPORK?
SORT OF A... SPOON CROSSED WITH A FORK.
POND, WE NEED TO DISABLE THE VROON WAR FLEET BEFORE TROUPE REACHES ST. PAUL'S CATHEDRAL, AND WE'RE RUNNING OUT OF TIME.

'WHERE'S RORY'?
ALL RIGHT, I'M GOING TO GET THIS OUT OF THE WAY NOW, BECAUSE LATER ON I THINK IT'S GOING TO BE EVEN MORE AWKWARD, BUT REALLY, HONESTLY...
...I AM NOT THE KING OF ENGLAND.
BUT YOUR CREDENTIALS WERE IMPECCABLE, YOUR MAJESTY.
PLEASE... STOP CALLING ME THAT.
AND LOOK AT YOUR BEARING! THAT ELEGANT NECK, THAT REGAL NOSE. OH, YOU'RE THE KING ALL RIGHT, I'D STAKE MY REPUTATION ON IT.
NO, JUST—HANG ON. I WAS SUPPOSED TO USE THE PSYCHIC PAPER TO PRETEND TO BE A MINOR ROYAL, THEN GET CLOSE TO HER MAJESTY SO I COULD PROTECT HER WHEN—
BOOM
—THIS HAPPENED.
WHAT THE DEVIL...?

WHO THE BLAZES ARE YOU?
AH... HOW QUICKLY THEY FORGET.
MY NAME IS REGINALD OFFORD TROUPE. AND THERE WAS A TIME WHEN YOU WOULD HAVE BENT YOUR KNEE AND CALLED ME 'YOUR LORDSHIP'. BUT YOU MAKE ONE FAUX PAS WITH AN AU PAIR, AND BEFORE YOU KNOW IT, YOU'RE EXILED TO SOME DREARY, BLOODY ROCK IN THE MEDITERRANEAN.
BUT ANYWAY...

...THAT'S ALL BEHIND ME NOW.
GENTLEMEN, ALLOW ME TO INTRODUCE THE VROON. AS YOU CAN SEE, THEY'RE ALIENS. MORE IMPORTANTLY, THEY'RE INCREDIBLY STRONG, VERY FIERCE, AND UTTERLY SINGLE-MINDED. I LIKE THEM A LOT.
WE'VE MADE A PACT. I OFFER THEM EARTH AS A BEACHHEAD IN THEIR WAR AGAINST THE NOORV, AND THEY HELP ME TAKE WHAT IS RIGHTFULLY MINE...

...NAMELY, THE THRONE.
WHERE IS HER MAJESTY?

ACTUALLY... I THINK I'M SORT OF THE KING NOW.
INDEED. THIS IS KING... SORRY, WHAT WAS YOUR NAME?
RORY.
KING RORY. THE FIRST.

EXCELLENT.
THEN OFF WITH YOUR HEAD.

So, to recap: an exiled royal has made an alliance with an alien race, Rory's the King of England, and the Doctor is stuck in a prison cell on the rock of Gibraltar. Got that? And I'm...

...what was I doing? Oh yeah...

ZZUMMMMM
KA-BOOM

DOCTOR? ARE YOU OKAY? DOCTOR?!

AMELIA POND, YOU ARE -KOFF- LITERALLY THE BEST THING THAT HAS EVER HAPPENED TO ME.

ALL RIGHT, THE SECOND BEST THING.
HELLO, OLD GIRL. FANCY MEETING YOU HERE.
DON'T MOVE!

HANDS IN THE AIR!
RIGHT, YES. HANDS IN THE AIR.
WHAT'S THAT YOU'RE HOLDING? LET'S SEE IT!

THIS? IT'S A SORT OF... WALKIE-TALKIE... THING. BUT I'D BE CAREFUL, BECAUSE IT'S STILL CONNECTED...

I'LL TAKE THAT AS A NO!

CONQUERORS OF VROON VANGUARD 'WARSTROKE', I AM VROON COMMANDER LETTMYR! RESPOND!
I'M AMY POND OF EARTH. WHAT'S UP?

BE AWARE, AMY POND OF EARTH, I WILL NOT HESITATE IN BLOWING YOU OUT OF THE SKY IF YOU DO NOT RELINQUISH CONTROL.
DO YOU OBEY?

I DO NOT. AND YOU LISTEN HERE, COMMANDER LEMON—
LETTMYR.
WHATEVER. WE'VE STAGED A COUP ON THIS WARSHIP WITH NOTHING BUT SPORKS, MOPS, AND... HAVE YOU SEEN BRAVEHEART?
NO.
WELL, I SORT OF DID MEL GIBSON'S SPEECH. IT WAS VERY STIRRING, AND IT TOTALLY WORKED.

SO I SEND THIS MESSAGE NOT TO YOU, BUT TO YOUR STAFF. TO EVERYONE TOILING AWAY IN THE KITCHENS, CLEANING UP YOUR MESS, SCRUBBING OUT YOUR CELLS... YOU CAN RISE UP! THROW OFF THE SHACKLES OF TYRANNY AND... AND...
...KICK SOME ARSE!

SHE IS A FOOL. LIEUTENANT, PREPARE THE PULSE CANNONS.

LIEUTENANT?

THEN OFF WITH YOUR HEAD.

THIS WOULD BE SUCH A STUPID WAY TO DIE.

OH, THANK GOD.

VWORP

VWORP!

AH YES, I SORT OF THOUGHT YOU MIGHT TRY THAT, SO I EXTENDED THE TARDIS FORCE FIELD TO PROTECT ME. ANYWAY, HELLO. RORY, WHY ARE YOU ON THE THRONE? NEVER MIND, WE'LL TALK ABOUT THAT LATER.

NOW, WHERE WAS I? OH YES...

...IT'S OVER, TROUPE. YOU'RE ***FINISHED***. LOWER YOUR WEAPONS, ALL OF YOU, AND I MIGHT LET YOU GO FREE.

LET US GO FREE?! YOU KNOW, I HEARD YOU WERE CLEVER, DOCTOR, BUT I HONESTLY THINK YOU MIGHT BE THE STUPIDEST MAN I'VE EVER MET.
CAPTAIN, KILL THE 'KING', AND ORDER YOUR FLEET TO BOMB LONDON FLAT. THE DOCTOR MIGHT SURVIVE, BUT HE'LL BE THE ONLY THING THAT WILL.
CAPTAIN? WHAT ARE YOU DOING?
I... I AM SENDING THE ORDER, BUT NO ONE RESPONDS. I DON'T UNDERSTAND...
ACTUALLY...
POP
...MAYBE I CAN EXPLAIN.

REGGIE, VROON CAPTAIN, MEET THE **UNITED WORKERS FRONT**. THEY'RE A BIT... HANG ON. RORY, WHY ARE YOU ON THE THRONE?
I... I SORT OF...
NEVER MIND, TELL ME LATER. WHERE WAS I? OH YEAH, THEY'RE **ANNOYED** BY THE CONDITIONS IN YOUR WAR FLEET, AND THEY'D LIKE A **WORD**.

YOU INTERFERING WITCH! WHY, I'LL—

DON'T EVEN THINK ABOUT IT, REG. I'VE GOT A **SPORK**.
OW!

AND I **KNOW** HOW TO USE IT.
I actually said that. That's what travelling with the Doctor does, turns you into a total quip-monster.

Anyway, that was that. The police came for Reggie Troupe, the United Workers Front took the Vroon soldiers away, and the Queen...
...Well, she's fine, Mum. Don't worry.

That was... let me see. Tuesday. Which was pretty mad...

...But just wait till you hear about Wednesday...
THE END.

ART GALLERY

Art by Mark Buckingham
Colors by Charlie Kirchoff

POLICE PUBLIC CALL BOX

Art by Ben Templesmith

Art by Mark Buckingham
Colors by Charlie Kirchoff

Art by **Matthew Dow Smith**
Colors by **Charlie Kirchoff**

Art by Mark Buckingham
Colors by Charlie Kirchoff

Art by Matthew Dow Smith
Colors by Charlie Kirchoff

Art by Mark Buckingham
Colors by Charlie Kirchoff

Art by **Paul Grist**
Colors by **Phil Elliott**